URBAN EDUCATION:
Crisis or Opportunity?

by

SHELDON MARCUS

and

PHILIP D. VAIRO

The Scarecrow Press, Inc.

Metuchen, N. J.   1972

Library of Congress Cataloging in Publication Data

Marcus, Sheldon, comp.
    Urban education.

    "An outgrowth of the summer institute in urban
education conducted by the Division of Urban Education
of Fordham University's School of Education in 1970 and
1971."
    CONTENTS: Education in a changing world, by J. Holt
--Changing power relationships in education, by
A. Shanker.--Education in an urban setting, by R. McCoy.
[etc.]
    1. Education, Urban--Addresses, essays, lectures.
2. Education, Urban--New York (City)--Addresses, lectures. I. Vairo, Philip D., joint comp. II. Title.
LC5131.M35   370.19'348   72-5467
ISBN 0-8108-0531-6

Dedicated to Beth and Jonathan, Mary and
Bonnie, and their Generation.

PREFACE

Each September witnesses a familiar American scene as millions of students and their teachers stream back to their classrooms in our cities. Also, thousands of beginning teachers assume their new posts. Most of these teachers are hopeful, idealistic, anxious, and perhaps even a little bit frightened. Regrettably, some teachers are hostile, frustrated, and sometimes even question the value of public education. This negativism stems from the fact that teachers are unfamiliar with the demands that teaching will make upon them in our urban centers.

That the ramifications of teaching in our cities go far beyond the classrooms and ivy-covered campus buildings may come as a startling surprise to the neophyte in the profession. As the preparation of our future citizens becomes more complex, the need for well-educated and sophisticated teachers and administrators becomes increasingly apparent. Many school personnel have found it difficult to understand and to keep abreast of the rapid changes in education that are taking place around them. It is certainly no surprise that parents should be caught up in the general confusion, problems, and misunderstandings of our urban educational system.

We hope that this book will shed some light on the problems which face both experienced and beginning teachers, school administrators, college professors, and parents. As college teachers, as former public school teachers, and as parents we trust that this book will serve as an invaluable introduction to urban education. The quality of education in our cities in the decade ahead will determine whether we shall have urban crises or urban opportunities.

We express our gratitude to our colleagues, friends, and above all to the students whose encouragement and support made this volume possible.

This book is an outgrowth of the summer institute in urban education conducted by the Division of Urban Education of Fordham University's School of Education in 1970 and 1971. Selected colleagues who did not participate in the urban institute were invited to submit relevant papers in order to broaden the scope of this manuscript.

Sheldon Marcus
Philip D. Vairo

CONTENTS

1. EDUCATION IN A CHANGING WORLD

Copyright 1971 by John Holt

When I was younger I believed in the magic power of words. I thought that if I could find the right words I could make people think the way I did. I no longer believe this. Now I strive only to illuminate minds by trying to throw a light on my own experience, hoping that sharing my experiences with other people would enable them to see things that they have not seen before or to see things in a new perspective.

My own style of thinking is concrete. One of my complaints about most so-called experts is that they live at far too high a level of abstraction. I think abstractions can be useful, but only if they come out of real life experiences. For example, I remember that prior to addressing a group of educators I was introduced by the host, who with very good intentions, said that he had always admired how clever I was at finding anecdotes to illustrate my theories or principles. I thanked him for the kind words, but I had to tell him that he really had it altogether backwards. I did not think up the anecdotes to illustrate the principles and theories. Rather, the principles and theories grow out of my experiences. On another occasion, a professor emeritus of education wrote a very perceptive and kindly review of How Children Learn, for the Harvard Review. But he said a surprising thing at the end of his review. He said that I had not acknowledged my debt to a huge number of educational theorists whose names he then proceeded to list. He went on to say that I would have people believe that my ideas about education and learning arose out of my experience in classrooms with children, and that this is a preposterous notion. He implied that you don't learn about children in a classroom, you learn about them out of books. I wrote him a letter in which I thanked him for the very nice review, but could not resist the temptation to put him straight on one point. I never read most of the works by the people he listed. I got my ideas about education, learning, children, growth and development,

1

whatever they may be worth, good or bad, as a result of
many encounters and experiences with children and then
reflecting on the experiences afterwards.   My mind works
concretely and, therefore, the best way for me to illuminate
my general thoughts about urban education may be to discuss
very concretely the question of reading--since this is certainly on everybody's mind.

In the last few years, people have begun to study in
a concentrated way the process by which children learn to
speak and understand their native tongue.   For a long time,
with very few exceptions, nobody thought this was worth in-
vestigating.   Today, however, a considerable number of
people have come to believe that it is important to look
very carefully at this aspect of learning which takes place
all over the world.   Everywhere people speak languages
which are about equally complicated.   Even primitive cultures may have quite complicated and difficult languages
but the young children still succeed in learning that
language.   Why?   My own feeling about this is that in
terms of quantities of information, abstractness, complexity, subtlety and ambiguity--every baby has to discover language, even before he learns it--the task of
discovering and learning one's language is a thousand
times harder than learning how to write and read it. But
with the exception of a very small percentage of very
seriously and congenitally deformed or malformed children,
everybody masters this task and they master it with virtually none of what we would call formal instruction. We
are not taught to speak.   In fact, at the conclusion of
How Children Fail, I quoted my dear friend and colleague,
Bill Hull, to the effect that if we taught children to
speak, they would never learn.   I think this is a profound truth.

Another concern which I have is on the use of words
which we use very widely in connection with schools.   For
example, we talk about basic skills, or the skills of reading.
I think the use of such words is an educational disaster and
that they should be purged from the vocabulary of education.
Of course, it is true that any act embodies a type of skill
and thus it is true that if I walk I am demonstrating the
skills of walking and if I whistle I am using the skills of
whistling.   But that is not how we learn things.   Whitehead,
in the Aims of Education, said that to try to separate the
skills of an activity from the activity itself is a disasterous
mistake.   But this is what educators try to do.   We did not

learn to walk by learning the skills of walking and then using
them to walk. We did not learn to talk by learning the skills
of speech and then using them to speak. We learn to speak
by speaking! Our first speech took place somewhere in the
first minute of birth as a cry. We didn't speak very well.
But from the beginning of our lives we were constantly using
our native potentiality for speech. We were using sounds to
communicate real meanings, real feelings, real wants and
real thoughts to real people from whom we got a real response. Our speech--and it was, at the beginning, crying,
gestures, and smiles--was intimately and inextricably connected with the rest of our life. We were not learning to
speak so that later on we could do things with it. Every
slight refinement or improvement in our ability to communicate our feelings or desires to other people brought us an
immediate reward, which was not praise or not smiles, but
an increase in our own powers of living. It was an advance
into the world. Furthermore, the people who surrounded
us when we were very young were also using speech. Their
speech was a part of our lives and one of the first things
we discovered was that these noises were somehow real and
important. They had something to do with our lives.
Thus, children who may be several months away from pro-
nouncing any recognizable word will already have learned
what I call "the music of speech."

Linguists who examine and study the beginning speech
of children are finding that a child learning to speak learns
a considerable amount of the grammar of his language even
before he actually utters any recognizable words. That is,
he has already grasped not just intonation and inflection,
but a great deal about the fundamental structure of the language. The first speech of children, though crude, is
grammatical. They use nouns nounishly and verbs verbishly.
Their model of the grammar of the language is a simple
and crude one, but it is an accurate one.

When discussing the early learning of speech in
children, it should be remembered that no two children
learn it in the same way. If we were to record children's
speech patterns to develop a chronological record of the
growth of a child's speech and vocabulary, we would find
that the growth of vocabulary, of syntax, of phrases, of
clauses and of structure is different for every child.
No two children explore and discover and absorb this great
territory of language in the same way. Yet, every child is
able to explore and master the difficult task of speech in his
own way.

This brings me to what I think is wrong with what we call the instruction of reading. It is taught as an abstract skill and as a general rule is separated from life. It is taught as something that must be learned now because later on it will be valuable. The rewards for learning to read are extrinsic rather than intrinsic--praise from the teacher or parents, receiving a gold star, being in the fast reading group in the class.

Another issue revolves around the education of illiterate adults. In a poverty area in the northeastern section of Brazil, one of the most destitute areas of the world, adults living in small villages, isolated from each other and from the world and in a culture virtually without the printed word, were taught how to read in an amazingly short period of time. How this was done bears very closely on the problem of teaching reading in our cities. The first thing that was done was to have as many men and women of these villages as possible attend a meeting to talk fully and freely about their problems, needs, difficulties, and tragedies. It was difficult, however, to get a representative meeting. The way these people had lived, their destitution, misery and hopelessness, had long since convinced them that what they said or even thought did not make any difference. So why bother to say or think it? They felt utterly incapable of changing the conditions of their lives. In many cases people were so afraid of what might happen to them if they did speak, that they now lived in a culture of demoralized silence. But the task of getting those people to attend meetings was carried on with great persistence and patience. At first, perhaps timidly and apologetically, but in time with greater conviction, people began to speak out. Word of this spread. More people attended meetings. This cycle continued until a point was reached where a room full of people gathered to talk seriously and with conviction about the real conditions of their lives.

During these meetings certain words began to constantly recur in their conversations. Words such as "landlords," "taxes," "water," and "disease." Words that were the central facts of their life. As these words appeared, these people were taught how to write these words. By writing them they could possess them and make them their own. That was the instructional method. Once this point was reached, a second process began, the instructional process. In a six- to eight-week period in evening classes, held after a back-breaking day's work, these formerly illiterate adults were brought to a literacy level comparable to the median literacy proficiency of the adult population of the United States. The expenditure per student required to achieve these results was approximately 25 dollars. In the United States we spend hundreds of dollars per pupil per year on the instructional process so that by the time a student is in the 6th or 7th grade he has had thousands of dollars spent on him. When we realize that very large numbers of these young people have not attained the level of literacy attained by these once illiterate adult men and women in these villages of South America, then we must conclude that we have not come to grips with the heart of the problem.

Let me shift the ground again. When I talked to groups of teachers about reading I have asked them to play a fantasy game with me. I said:

> Let's imagine that you are now living in a culture in which, for various reasons, it has been decided that children should not read until after the age of ten. So your problem as a teacher and as a custodian of young people is to make sure that they do not read before then. So what will you do in order to achieve this goal? You can't blindfold them and you can't shut them up in a box. Do you think, in fact, that any method would work?

Most teachers say they don't think they could prevent children from reading. I agree with them. I think we would have many more readers and fewer of what we call reading problems, if reading instruction were not the charge of the schools. Schools do not teach children how to talk, throw a baseball, ride a bicycle, skip rope, but almost all children learn how to do these things. I would say that we would have vastly more readers and better readers if for every child under the age of ten reading were made illegal. We could not prevent children from learning to read. The average child who lives in an urban environment, rich or poor, sees everyday, outside of school, two to five hundred printed words. He sees thousands of words on television every week. Some researchers made a word count of the comic books that children like to read and found that they have a vastly larger vocabulary, for the most part, than can be found in the books that they are given to read at school. I do not think there is any way in the world to prevent children surrounded by printed words from reading. If

reading were illegal, children would find ways to pass on this
illicit knowledge, just as they find ways to pass on to each
other kinds of knowledge that adults don't want them to know,
including the word which is never misspelled. At least, I
have never seen it misspelled. But no adult, let alone
teacher, taught all those people how to spell that word.

One of the things that I have come to feel is that it
isn't what we tell people but how we treat them that truly in-
fluences their behavior. Now the spoken message given to
children about reading is that reading is important and that
reading is fun. It seems to me, however, that there are
hidden messages, which we express in our behavior, in our
attitudes, and in our anxieties that contradict this. For example, we adults make clear to children that if we didn't
make them read, they never would. We also imply that we
want children to read regardless of whether the child wants
to learn. Finally, we say that children are so stupid and
the task of reading so immense and complicated that unless
we show them, step by tiny step, exactly how to do it, they
will never learn. Many children, of course, simply pay no
attention to those hidden messages. They look around them
and note that other people have learned how to read, many
of them before they ever attended school. Other children
don't teach themselves to read before they get to school but
they do teach themselves to read in school, along with filling
out the workbooks and circling the initial consonants. And
perhaps they do it in spite of adults. There are, however,
a great many children who take these hidden messages very
seriously. They hear adults say, "We are going to teach
you to read. We are going to make you read whether you
want to or not." They reply with "Oh you are, are you?
We will see about that."

Children are powerless people, but if they feel themselves in a struggle with adults they will look for whatever
weapons they can find. All of a sudden they find themselves
with power because they can make adults turn handsprings by
refusing to perform specific tasks, such as reading. I have
tried to teach reading to children who have decided that they
were not going to learn because adults were trying to make
them learn or because they were in a power struggle with
somebody at home and they were going to get even with them
by refusing to learn. This is a problem, although not a
reading problem. There are other children who think,
"Reading is terribly difficult. I'll never be able to do it."
And to the extent that a child feels that way, learning to

read is terribly hard. He is, in fact, going to have trouble
learning how to read. Finally, I think a lot of children have
come to think of learning to read, as indeed of all things in
school, as a somewhat passive process in which things are
done to them or put into them. They sit and wait for people
to give them learning. But children can't learn anything that
way and if one has that kind of pupil, there is no way he can
be taught. Learning is profoundly an act on the part of the
learner. It is not a transmission. So if a child feels that
reading is something that he is going to be given by a teacher, he is not going to learn how to read.

But suppose we were to make reading illegal for
children. Imagine a teacher saying to children, "Listen, if
I catch you reading you are going to be in real trouble."
That would be the spoken message. But the hidden message
would be that reading is fascinating. And the second hidden
message would be that reading is so easy and children are
so smart that if the teacher turns his back for one second,
children will learn to read. The child senses that reading
must be great and it must be easy to learn, so he will go
out and learn to read. Nothing will stop him.

Writing and reading are a form of speech, and no
child is going to be very interested in mastering this kind of
speech, in learning how to write his words, or in reading
other people's words, unless he feels that what he can say
is important and makes a difference. If we don't help a
child to feel that his ideas, needs, hopes, fears, wishes,
and dreams are important, then he will never be educated.
We can pile methods, texts and audio-visual devices right up
to the ceiling, but the person who feels that his thoughts and
his words are worthless is not going to be interested in
various ways of expressing them. What I'm saying in general terms, therefore, is that there is no such thing as an
education that does not grow out of the center of people's
lives as they experience it. I think one of the reasons why
poor children--Black, Irish, Italian, Chinese, Scandinavian,
Jewish or whatever--have always had a difficult time in
school, is because by and large the schools have treated
them as if their background, their family, their culture, their
neighborhood, their habits and their ways of talking were a
kind of disease from which they had to be cured before learning could take place.

This approach is indeed more than a mistake, it is a
disaster! We must legitimize the life and the existence of

each student and make him feel that where he is and what he thinks and what he wants to say is important; that this will be the best and the only starting place for his further exploration of the world. If we can do this, we will be well on the way toward solving the educational problems that now look so difficult.

2. CHANGING POWER RELATIONSHIPS IN EDUCATION

by Albert Shanker

It is very unusual for people in the field of education to discuss power. If one thinks back ten years, it would be difficult to find an essay, speech, or book on the question of power groupings in education. Instead, there were books and discussions about organizations in education, about the superintendents' role, teacher associations, school boards and state legislatures. But the very notion that the educational process depended on raw power was never discussed. The fact remains, however, that there were long periods of time when there was a struggle between school boards and superintendents, and that this struggle, which continues today, centers on whether school boards have a right to interfere with administrative functions and whether the administrator is making educational policy rather than implementing school board policy.

The New York State Educational Conference Board has represented the coming together of a formidable educational-political machine that has been operating from the 1920's until very recently and which is in the process of disintegrating at the present time. While it is true that school systems are operated by their local boards, the control of education from a legal point of view has been in the hands of the state--state legislatures, state boards of education, boards of regents, departments of education, or state commissioners of education. To a large extent what local groups and school boards could do was dependent upon the state legislature or rulings of the state commissioner of education. The power struggle that went on in the field of education during the past decades involved the development of a formula to distribute state aid to education. In essence, what was at stake was billions of dollars which were being distributed. When there was so much money involved there was bound to be a good deal of fighting over its distribution, and there indeed was. But the fighting was behind closed doors. The New York State Educational Conference Board was a typical power structure, designed to work out within the group, which organization was

9

to get what and how much. The organizations making up the
Board were groups such as the New York State School Boards
Association, the New York State Congress of Parents, the
State-Wide Committee for Better Schools, the various New
York State administrative associations, the New York State
Teachers' Association and the Public Education Association.
The New York State Educational Conference Board, year after
year, sat down and worked out a preliminary plan that it
would approve.   It was the group that the governor and the
legislative leadership consulted.   They said: "What is it that
you really want?   What things are you willing to drop?"

There were a number of interesting things about this
arrangement.   First, the money to operate these state structures basically came from the New York State Teachers'
Association, which had the financial resources because there
were 50, 000 to 70, 000 teachers in the association, and whatever monies were needed to operate generally came from
this broad based organization of teachers.   Despite the financial support emanating from the teachers organization, it
was controlled by the local superintendents, who, because
they were in touch with parents and legislators, were able to
mobilze support and persuade the legislators.   During this
period the local teachers' association at the grassroots level
was also under the control of the local superintendent.   Both
teachers and administrators held membership in the National
Educational Association, and they were considered to be so-
called educational partners.   Until the late 1950's, there was
no collective bargaining, teacher strikes were very limited,
and binding teacher contracts did not exist.   The Teachers'
Association was by and large acknowledged as the only viable
lobbying group for teachers.   The parents groups included in
this organization were there in order to create the image
that "we're all in this group together because we believe in
quality education. "   The notion that people were fighting over
money was totally submerged.   To an outsider it seemed
that the New York State Educational Conference Board was a
cooperative enterprise composed of teachers, parents, school
board members, principals, and all those interested citizens
who believe that schools needed additional funds.   Of course,
beneath the surface of tranquility, there was tremendous
fighting going on between the various factions to see who was
to get the largest share of the appropriations.

Appearances to the contrary, there were certain
groups that were not represented on the New York State Education Conference Board.   For example, no representative

from New York City, or from any of the big cities in New
York State was part of the Board, primarily because the
Board contained few member teachers from New York City
and the other large cities in the state. Generally, the big
city administrators did not join statewide associations. The
State School Board Association was an organization in which
each school board has one vote, so that the New York City
school system, regardless of its size, had very little power
in the School Board Association. Essentially, the groups
that made the decisions in education for New York State and
many other states up until the 1950's were rural-dominated
and acted as though they were not concerned with power but
only with doing good for education. In actuality, they were
a political group that operated against urban communities and
the minority groups who inhabited these areas. Blacks,
Puerto Ricans, and other minority groups had no power representation. The real power groups met with the governor,
the regents, the leadership of the legislature, and the state
commissioner of education. Happily, for a number of reasons, this pattern started breaking up in the 1950's. Now,
rural areas no longer dominate state legislatures. The Supreme Court's one-man-one-vote decision, the movement of
citizens away from rural American into urban and suburban
society, the emergence of a strong civil rights movement in
the decade from 1955-1965 that focused on the problems of
minorities suffering discrimination, and the emergence of a
strong, militant teacher movement all contributed to the destruction of the old structure. The New York State Conference Board is no longer the exclusive group that sits with
the governor and with the leaders of the legislature to decide
on educational matters. As a matter of fact, on the very
crucial New York City decentralization controversey in 1970,
I doubt that they were even consulted. In a number of recent questions in the state legislature they were on the outside. They represent an old group that is declining in power
while new power groups are emerging.

This change was hastened by the fact that teachers
started to become militant, demanding collective bargaining
contracts and going out on strike. Those actions meant that
they were no longer in partnership with either administrators
or school boards. The State School Boards Association
would say, "We used to think that teachers stood for all the
nice and good things that we were working for with the citizens on a state-wide level. But now that we see that
teachers are just interested in higher salaries and better
working conditions for themselves, we no longer want to work
with them. "

The money the teachers formerly contributed to these
power structures was no longer made available to them because the teachers' union and the teachers' association were
so busy fighting each other over the question of collective
bargaining that they had little, if any, money left over to
give to these lobbying groups. Most of the money was spent
on conducting strikes and in trying to win a collective bargaining election. In the beginning of the 1960's, teachers
said, "Look, there has been politics in the schools for years.
There are people who are getting money while we are not.
There are people whose conditions are improving while ours
are not. "

At the very same time, black, Puerto Rican, Mexi-
can-American, poor white and other groups came forward
and said, "Our children are not getting enough money allocated for their education. Our school buildings are decay-
ing. There is not an adequate distribution of experienced
teachers in inner city schools. "

Everybody started coming forth--teachers, administrators, parents, minority groups; they echoed a common
line. "We used to think of school as a good place where
everybody was doing things that were good for children. We
now see that there is a lot of fighting going on the inside,
with each group trying to obtain financial gain for itself
while ignoring the educational process. "

It became rather popular during this period of time
for people to engage in an open struggle. Teachers, for the
first time, were willing to stand up and be counted. Before
that, if teachers stood up to ask for a salary increase, they
would do it very sheepishly, saying "it's not that I want the
money, but that it would be better for the schools if my
salary was higher. " It had been drilled into teachers for
years that if they were interested in more money for themselves, it would mean that they were not interested in the
children. Until very recently, for a teacher to say openly
that he was interested in money, indicated that he was
against the real interests of the children. But in the late
1950's and early 1960's teachers changed their thinking on
this issue, and justifiably so. Nobody assumes that because
a doctor makes huge amounts of money that he is not interested in his patients. As a matter of fact, people would not
go to a doctor who earned a teacher's salary. They would
think that there are probably good reasons for his not having
a high income. So, too, nobody refrains from going to a

lawyer because he earns a great deal of money. If you do not go to a high-priced lawyer, it is because you can't afford to pay his fees. But if he is earning a good deal of money, it's probably because he is a good lawyer.

So it was that teachers openly decided that they wanted to improve their economic status and to gain a voice in the decision-making process in education. Teachers simply said: "We want more for ourselves." This is true around the country. Many major conflicts emerged during that period of time, as a result of the growing power of teacher unions and let me state unequivocally that I now consider the National Education Association a union. It may not want to call itself that, but they go on strike, and they negotiate contracts. They handle grievances and grievance procedures. The NEA looks like a union and talks like a union, but if they want to call themselves something else, that is all right. But if they behave like the auto workers, the steel workers and the garment workers, which they do in terms of where most of their money and energy is directed, even if they do not want to say the dirty word, "union," that is what they really are.

Teachers' unions now negotiate for higher salaries, improved pension programs, and welfare plans. These are the big money items in any contract, and as teachers negotiated for them, they came into great conflict with school boards and the political authorities, particularly the school boards. This occurred because all of the money that was allocated for these areas obviously could not be used by a board of education to do other things that they might have wished to do. The board of education no longer became the only, or for that matter, even the chief policy maker in the school system. They could not make policy without the money to implement it. If money had to be taken from funds earmarked to repair buildings, and used instead to raise teacher salaries, then essentially the policy-making power of school boards was being severely limited by collective bargaining and negotiations.

In addition to higher salaries and improved pension and welfare benefits, teachers also came to demand smaller class sizes, and professional preparation time during the working day, so that they could unwind after the battles of the classroom. The concept of "preparation" was imposed by the school board in order to create good public relations with parents who resent schools and seeing teachers having free

time.   They say the teacher already has a short work year,
and now he wants an even shorter work day.   However, this
same parent, when she has to take care of her own three
kids on a Saturday or Sunday, complains that she cannot stand
it.   When her husband comes home from work she would say,
"Now, you take care of the children. "   This parent walks
into a school and deeply resents the fact that a teacher who
is with 30 children for a whole day has 30 or 40 minutes to
relax.   The concept of preparation time, therefore, is
really a public relations device.   The teachers are not re-
laxing.   They are preparing to deal with children!   The
elimination of non-teaching chores and the various secre-
tarial, police, and monitorial type of functions such as pa-
trolling the yards, cafeterias, and hallways, and pushing
students out of the bathrooms, have also brought teachers
into conflict with both school boards and administrators.   Today the typical principal of a school will say:

> Certainly I think that classes ought to be smaller,
> but I do not want to have an absolute maximum
> imposed on me that says no more than 30 children
> in a class.   After all, I am the principal, and I
> am paid to run this school.   I only have a certain
> number of teachers and ... I may believe there
> ought to be one or two classes of 40 children so
> that I can have a teacher to handle another group
> of six to eight children.   Unless I have that flexi-
> bility to create some large classes at one end so
> that I can create some small ones at the other,
> then I am being paid to do what I am not able to
> do.

As far as clerical and other chores are concerned,
the principal will say, "All this costs money.   We have to
hire school aides to do this kind of work.   Also, some of
the aides may not be able to handle the cafeteria or some of
the hall patrols.   Having non-teachers do this work will have
a detrimental effect on discipline within the school. "   Discussing preparation time, the principal will usually say: "If
the teachers have preparation time, I can't do the things that
I need done as a principal. "   Thus, there is tremendous conflict as to whether preparation time really belongs to the
teacher or whether it is his at the discretion of the principal.

Another area of conflict is the participation period in
elementary schools.   That time is created by sending a
second teacher into a room to work with the children while

the homeroom or regular teacher is getting her preparation
period. That means that once you decide on having preparation time, you are also making a policy decision. To a
certain degree you are deciding to departmentalize the elementary school. Administrators and school board members
on this question have replied:

> The union has a right to demand time for its
> people but it cannot force us to operate a school
> in a particular way. In this demand the teachers
> are compelling us to make an educational decision.
> Is it good for children in the first, second, third,
> and fourth grades to have different teachers com-
> ing in and out of the room for one period or two
> periods? Can children at this age relate to that
> many teachers? Can the homeroom teacher who
> is with them all the time do a better job than the
> teacher who comes in just once a week?

Conflict arises on the question of whether things are
good for children and whether in the negotiation of a contract the teachers are not really making decisions going far
beyond the negotiation of a particular working condition by
limiting the right of administrators and the school board to
run their school. Take the "ideal" principal of a school.
By "ideal" I mean that he really wants to do the best for
every child and every teacher in the school. To accomplish
this the principal must evaluate each teacher in the school
and decide how that teacher's skills can be best utilized. It
is the principal's job to match the teacher with the various
tasks that have to be performed within a school. But what
actually happens when teachers are assigned to the various
positions inside of the school--from a more difficult class to
a slow class, to a bright class, to an administrative job, to
a series of chores which are very unpleasant or difficult?
The teachers rarely see the principal. The principal is
somebody "speaking from heaven" and trying to do a good
job in matching each person with the particular job they can
do best. Yet, some teachers will feel that the principal is
giving all sorts of favors to his friends in the school. They
may believe that he is "punishing" the teacher who spoke up
at a faculty conference last year or the teacher who refused
to attend a lunch hour conference. In other words, like all
human beings, when teachers obtain some positions within a
school, they believe the jobs were assigned equitably. When
they are assigned to unpleasant positions, they generally do
not believe the decisions were made on the basis of justice.

The personality factor obviously cannot be ignored in assigning teachers to positions and often there is an attempt by the administrator to reward or punish his teachers. There are politics and patronage within every school. Teachers, however, through their collective bargaining contracts, have succeeded in building systems of rotation--that is, systems of objective qualifications to protect themselves and negate favoritism. Basically, teachers have tried to say that when principals make the difficult choice assignments in a school that they do so according to objective criteria. This has caused tremendous friction between teachers and administrators. After all, the administrator looks at himself in the mirror in the morning and says, "What am I being paid for? I'm being paid to give certain people certain tasks because I know their capabilities and all of a sudden along comes a contract which says I can no longer do that."

The implementation of grievance procedures indeed shakes the entire power structure of a school and school system at its foundation. Implementation, however, is not easy to accomplish. Rather, it is like going into court and trying to get justice. A teacher goes to the principal and says, "You have violated the contract. You have taken away the following time from me. I, therefore, have a grievance." The principal is now confronted with a problem. If he says, "You are right." to that particular teacher, he will be concerned that many more teachers are going to start coming to see him with their grievances. He thinks teachers may get out of control if their requests are frequently approved. On the other hand, if he says "NO" then what happens? The teacher goes on to the district superintendent who, no matter what else he does, is going to be very angry at the principal. Imagine the district superintendent sitting in at a grievance hearing for three hours discussing whether or not this particular teacher should have had a duty-free lunch period. The superintendent has many more important things to do. At the very least, he will privately ask the principal, "What's the matter with you? Can't you handle your own problems? Do you realize that I have other things that are overwhelming me and I have to sit here discussing whether a teacher should have a duty-free lunch period?" So the first thing that happens to the principal when he goes to the central administration is that he is "reamed" for not being able to handle the problem at his own level.

Now, the district superintendent has a problem. Does he back up the principal? Most of the time he must. Otherwise, he feels that the chain of command is broken and the morale of his principals will dissipate. But if he does support his principal, the arbitrator at the next step may overrule him and support the teacher. One can see that the existence of grievance procedure, in addition to providing justice for teachers, also brings about changes in power relationships in the school structure.

Teachers have recently exhibited a great deal of concern about their economic status and they will continue to do so in the future. But they will also become more involved in professional matters. Until quite recently, the word "professionalism" was used in the field of education in a meaning opposite to its true meaning. The word "professional" was used as a stick. If the teacher did not do what the principal, parents' association, superintendent, or the local school board wanted him to do, these people would say, the way you say to a child, "Ah, ah, you're a bad boy; you are very unprofessional." "Unprofessional" meant that you were not doing what the administration wanted you to do. The "professional" was a person who was merely supposed to be obedient. He had to listen to his principal. He had to follow orders. He had to get his records in on time. He had to see that the bulletin board was always up on time. The "professional" was the person who did not ask questions; who did not "rock the boat." Actually that type of "professional" was as unprofessional as one could possibly imagine. That meaning of the word "professional" is a distortion. A professional is really an expert who because he is an expert has a fairly high degree of decision-making power and is relatively unsupervised. Doctors, lawyers, dentists, and others are people that one would classify as professionals. Because their skills are recognized and certified by an impartial board, they are essentially unsupervised. This does not mean that the profession does not develop certain checks on teachers and that there are no ways of removing professionals if they are incompetent. Since teachers have been told that they are professionals, they are now demanding the common expectations of professional courtesy enjoyed by their colleagues in other professions.

There are a number of other reasons for the change in the relationship between teachers and administrators. If one goes back three or four decades, there was a tremendous gap in the professional preparation between teachers and administrators. In those days, prospective teachers attended teacher training schools for one or two years. The principal

was one of the few college graduates on the faculty. Back
in the late 1940's when I was completing three years of
college and thinking of leaving before actually graduating, I
applied for a job in North Dakota. I was offered an acting
superintendency. At that time the teachers in that particular
area of North Dakota either were high school graduates or
had completed one year of college and/or teacher training
school. At that time, principals were people with two years
of college and superintendents usually had completed three
years of college or held a college degree. But now, of
course, we have a situation where many teachers are actually
more qualified and better educated, especially in their own
subject, than are their principals. So now teachers turn
around and raise the question, "Who gives the administration
the right to come into my room to tell me whether I am doing right or wrong when I am much more an expert in my
particular field than he is?" Furthermore, we are now, of
course, part of a world-wide movement stressing group participation. One sees this phenomenon reflected in the student
movements, in the organization of teachers, and civil service
personnel. There is a general mood of rejection of authority
in our society. Teachers are now following the lead of many
segments of society in this respect.

Teachers are rejecting the archaic concepts of general supervision and administration which they were taught in
universities. Most of the recent research which has been
done in the last five to ten years has raised serious questions about something that we all used to believe--namely,
that somebody knew what was "good" in education. People
used to think that educators knew what was right and wrong
with curriculum; that supervisors knew who was a good
teacher and who was a poor teacher. Theoretically, the
supervisor was supposed to be the staff member who was
knowledgeable in teacher evaluation. We indeed know very
little about whether one curriculum is better than another or
one particular teaching method is superior to another. Therefore, when the supervisor walks into the teacher's class to
observe, the teacher has serious reservations whether the
supervisor can really be constructive and assist the teacher.
Of course, teachers should not be too joyous about this because if we say we are all ignorant about what we are doing,
this gives local parents the right to walk into a school and
dictate to us. Therefore, I do not want to celebrate the
existence of this state of ignorance.

I believe that education is at crossroads at this time.

It is possible that we will continue with the present struggles
and that there will be greater state and federal control of education as well as more generous financial assistance to the
schools. This is not, however, inconsistent with a very high
degree of local decision-making in certain areas. Another
alternative, which some of the Canadian provinces have taken,
is to establish state-wide school systems. People are also
talking about basic services, including education, becoming
state-wide, with collective negotiations taking place on a
state-wide level with some variations for local considerations
such as the cost of living. With a growing movement toward
national assessment and with national aid there will likely be
more federal control in this area. Instead of having greater
state and federal monies and control, we will have a complete
dismantling of the public education system. Supporters of this
belief utilize three popular themes:

> I am the state government. I am the federal
> government. I am sick and tired of everybody--
> civil rights groups, teachers, school boards, su-
> perintendents, and parents--coming to me and con-
> stantly saying, 'We need more money. We need
> more buildings. We have to do this. We have to
> do that.' I'm tired of giving. I just don't want to
> give anymore.

Can this giving be stopped? The answer is possibly.
One such method of achieving this is known as "decentralization." One day I had a long talk with an individual who supported the concept of decentralization. At the end of that
talk I asked him, "But do you really think if New York is
divided into 30, 60, 100, or 150 school districts, that Johnny
who isn't reading now, will be able to read?" He said: "No,
but they won't blame me or you if Johnny isn't reading. They
will throw out their local school board members and elect
another school board. We will be safe." I do not want to
over-simplify by stating that this is the only reason some
people advocate decentralization, but a very strong decentralization law takes many educational responsibilities from the
federal and state governments and shifts them to local districts. Many local school boards have been meeting with the
central board seeking ways to obtain funds. Each district
thinks it should get more money than the other districts. One
points to the next individual who is saying, "They have too
much. Take away half of their money and give it to us."
The whole power struggle now shifts. Each urban community
now fights to get its share of state and federal monies from

the same central board which has the same amount of money
to dispense as it had before the passage of the decentralization law.

The second area of concern which is surfacing is performance contracting. In Texarkana, on the Texas and
Arkansas border, a private corporation was given a contract
which stipulated that they would get "X" number of dollars
for each child that improved two years in reading within a
certain period of time. A very interesting thing happened
as a result of that experiment. Students had learned to
function very well with machines, but they felt very ill at
ease with other people in the classroom. As the program
came to an end, the students were given plaid stamps for
every correct answer they attained, so that the good students
went home with radio and television sets at the end of the
week. Most teachers were given plaid stamps and stock options in the company on the basis of how their pupils achieved. The program was pronounced a great success until a
number of students walked into class and looked at the test
they were supposed to take and said, "These are the exact
questions we have been working on for the last three weeks!
Isn't that terrific. " To put it simply, there was some dis-
honesty in the administration of the program. But even more
interesting is the reaction of the Office of Economic Opportunity when the irregularities were discovered. The Office
of Economic Opportunity immediately gave 50 more performance contracts around the country to various companies to do
something similar to what was done in this little Texas border
town. The Office of Economic Opportunity said that since
this experiment was disrupted by irregularities, they would
now have to test it on a wide-spread basis in places where
they could get honest results.

Basically, the contract performance is very simple.
Local school districts contract with a company--Xerox, IBM,
General Dynamics, and so forth. Performance contracting
takes the responsibility for educating children away from the
state and federal government. It says to the parents of local
schools, "Look, if your school is not doing well right now,
switch from Xerox to IBM. Perhaps they have a better
thing. "

A third area which is developing considerable interest
is the voucher system, whereby each child's parents would
be given a sum of money to be used if they so wish to enter
their children in a private or parochial school of their choice.

Teachers may establish their own school for which vouchers would be acceptable. In other words, each child would be given a GI bill of rights and consequently this would eliminate the educational monopoly the public schools now have. If people are unhappy with their local public school, they can take their voucher to another public school that will accept it or to a private or parochial school. If parents are unhappy with the education their children are receiving, they simply take their vouchers and select the product of their choice which is available on the academic market.

In conclusion, I think that we are at a crossroad and the issue is basically whether we are going to continue to have a publicly supported educational system or not. Government at the state and national level must recognize that they cannot ignore the massive problems in education which face our nation.

We must recognize that we have never satisfactorily educated the poor minority groups. Our society has discriminated against urban areas. The federal government must exercise the same kind of concern and leadership for solving the problems of education as they exercised in creating a nuclear bomb or developing some other type of implement for war. If the government fails in this task, we will have chaos.

If we are to put together something resembling a golden age of education, where we have both the money and other resources that are necessary to educate our citizens, we will have to rebuild the political coalition which used to exist between labor and civil rights groups. We must try to put together the kind of national commitment that will provide the impetus for educating the poor. This is a must if society based on equality for all is to flourish. If public education fails to educate the inner city masses, then this nation is doomed to extinction in the near future.

3. EDUCATION IN AN URBAN SETTING

by Rhody McCoy

Let me attempt to do the impossible, that is, to present what transpired from 1967-71 in the public schools of New York City, with special emphasis on occurrences in Ocean Hill-Brownsville.

The parents in the Ocean Hill-Brownsville area of Brooklyn had to send their children to schools that failed to educate. The original district, where Ocean Hill-Brownsville is presently located, for a number of years had probably the lowest academic performance of any school district in New York City. So the parents decided to pressure for the creation of an experimental district, in which they would control what transpired in the schools. During the years prior to the actual establishment of the experimental district, boycotts, demonstrations, and social unrest were daily occurrences. People were unhappy with the schools.

We, the community of Ocean Hill-Brownsville, decided to try to do something about this kind of a situation. We refused to accept the same bill of goods that they had been accepting for years. We no longer believed it when we were told that everything was going to be all right. Instead, we did things that had to be done for our clientele. For instance, we appointed the first Puerto Rican principal in New York City and the first Chinese principal in the United States. That's significant because if educators use psychological terms that describe the importance of self-image and success models, then, very obviously, the students need to see success models from their own groups. Therefore, we undertook the task of creating some visible successes and illustrating visible changes that people could support and have confidence in.

Let me take one particular school in Ocean Hill-Brownsville. This school is situated on a little street just off a busy thoroughfare. It was built 92 years ago. We have tried to give it back to the City as a landmark; but

22

somehow, or another, they have refused to accept it. When
I arrived as unit administrator and visited this school I
could not find the children because it was so dark and gloomy.
There were times when if more than three electrical appli-
ances were used, all the fuses blew.   There is a very unusual architectural design on the first floor.   There are
three classrooms, and in order to get to the third one, you
had to go through the first two.   The building does not have
a library, lunch facilities or adequate plumbing.   It is almost
inconceivable that children attended this school.

The parents, despite strenuous efforts, failed to get
this school into some sort of livable condition.   At that point
some parents suggested burning the school to the ground.
This action would dramatically bring to the attention of the
people, politicans and Board of Education the deplorable conditions in the school.

Every year the school received an allotment for library books of approximately $10,000.   Of course, library
books were ordered simply because it was a state law, but
we had no place to put them.   We could have used the money
for something we desperately needed.   In my opinion, what
happened in the school is typical of what is happening in
most schools in the urban setting across this country.   In
Chicago, for example, in one school, on a very cold winter
day, every window in the building was broken.   The broken
windows clearly indicate that its clientele have rejected the
school.   When we came into Ocean Hill in 1967, we found in
the school yards just about everything imaginable, including
discarded automobiles as well as broken glass and debris.

It is difficult to categorize the various activities that
took place in Ocean Hill.   For example, the large Puerto
Rican pupil population in Ocean Hill were being taught and
tested in English.   We decided that in order for these people
to begin to grasp the basic tools of education that they had to
receive what we call bi-lingual education.   That decision was
reached by the parents, a group of Puerto Rican parents who
requested this of the governing board, and educational leaders of the community.   All agreed that such a program
should be put into operation.   As a result we established a
pilot program in bi-lingual education.   First, we went to
Puerto Rico to recruit 32 teachers to come to Ocean-Hill to
teach in our bi-lingual program school.   We subsequently ran
into some obstacles with the Board of Education and the
Board of Examiners.   They went down to Puerto Rico, tested

these people in English, and failed 30 out of the 32. The
fact is, however, that we wanted them to teach Spanish.
Then it was suggested to us that these Puerto Rican teachers
would put other teachers out of work. Amazing as it may
seem, one member of the Board of Examiners wanted to
know if they were United States citizens. This gives you an
idea of the mentality of those who opposed us. Nevertheless
the bi-lingual programs funded by the Federal government in
Ocean Hill had great success. We also introduced the Montessori Method into our schools, a method which is still kept
out of other New York City schools. When I keep referring
to "We," I am talking about parents. Parents who are saying let us be involved in decision making. If you are appre-
hensive about giving parents control of education, let me say
that they just don't run down the street and fly into an office
and demand a program. They work very closely with the
school authorities; as professional educators it is our function to provide them with sufficient background information,
and this we did quite successfully.

Various kinds of reading programs were examined including programmed materials and many other commercially
produced products. The parents finally decided this material
was inadequate and that if educators were not competent to
develop curricula materials, they would try to design and
develop their own educational programs, particularly in the
area of reading. So we set up a task force, in each of the
schools consisting of parents, teachers, administrators, and
in the secondary schools to include students. The task forces
produced such outstanding materials and programs that the
Board of Education refused to evaluate the results it produced, because its success would have embarrased them.

In Ocean Hill-Brownsville we defined very carefully
what our goals and objectives were and we met those goals.
We were concerned with the teacher shortage and the high
rate of teacher absenteeism. The UFT contract with the
Board of Education limited class size. Assume that the contractual obligation for class size is 21. When you have 20
percent of your school's teachers absent on an average day,
the class size has little, if any, meaning because you place
students into larger classrooms in order to get teacher
coverage. This is a standard practice in many school systems. A more recent union contract guarantees a teacher
payment every time he gives up a preparation period to
cover classrooms. If the preparation periods are that important, how can one put a price tag on them? Why give them
up?

We introduced a paraprofessional program addressing the kinds of problems created when students do not receive a quality education because of the absence of so many teachers.   In Ocean Hill we created a paraprofessional cadre of some 735 parents to overcome the problem of teacher absence.   Unfortunately, many people believe that in the Black and Puerto Rican communities, ignorance, apathy, and poverty handicap such a program.   What we did was to make a community survey, and we found large percentages of black mothers and Puerto Rican mothers who had finished high school and had one or more years of college.   Using this community human resource, additional strength was added to our schools in the areas of library and in teaching reading.   Prior to that time if a parent attended an Ocean Hill PTA meeting, she would find five or six people--and that was considered to be a crowd.   But when community people began getting involved in the local PTA meetings, parent attendance ran from 125 to 150, and when a community meeting was held attendance ran from 500 to 700 people.

This new esprit de corps was readily demonstrated by the principals, who were meeting with the teachers and by parents working together seven days a week.   One more interesting activity involved a visit by parents, teachers, and administrators to England to see the British Infant School. Upon their return, both the school and community people spent the remainder of the summer setting up three model programs.   The concept of partners in education was born. The idea that only school people know what is best for the children was proven to be outdated.

The fact that the private sector is entering the field of education via contract accountability and by the creation of voucher systems in California, is an indication that public education is not functioning.   We need the help of parents to be successful.   There are too many people who believe that when the local people take control, teachers will lose their jobs.   This does not make too much sense.   Actually, control of the schools rests in the pocketbook.   Since community people in large cities do not have control over the funds, then obviously they will not have control over the personnel in the district.   At one point, the New York State legislature said that Ocean Hill could not use money appropriated by the state to increase teachers' salaries.   This illustrated the low level of the intelligence of the representatives in Albany because in New York City individual local school districts do not have the authority to raise teacher salaries.

A major problem in Ocean Hill-Brownsville involved
the question of utilizing money to renovate ancient school
buildings.   The cost of renovating such a building was about
$425, 000.   This is a lot of money.   Yet, in most of New
York City,   blacks and Puerto Ricans were usually excluded
from bidding on such contracts.   In Ocean Hill-Brownsville,
however, we gave our renovation contracts to black and
Puerto Rican companies.

We tried to get people involved in developing a program for our schools.   For example, it was suggested that
welfare recipients be taken off the rolls and be given an
opportunity to obtain a high school diploma, and hopefully,
get a chance to enter a college.   But we ran into trouble
when the Board of Education agreed to pay people only $1. 75.
The Board of Education said that under civil service law, in
order for a person to get $3. 00 an hour, he has to have a
minimum of one and one-half years of college.   If the people
in Ocean Hill could meet those requirements, they would not
have been unemployed to begin with.   Stupid regulations such
as this one made it almost impossible for us to spend the
money at our disposal and to produce educational miracles.

For ten years minority groups in New York City have
been told that integrated education and the integrated setting
is best for blacks and Puerto Ricans.   To be perfectly
frank, it is simply not working in any state in this country.
As a matter of fact the Constitution has nine amendments
that are designed for the protection of minorities.   It took
the blacks, Puerto Ricans, and Mexicans ten years to discover that this concept of integration is a fraud.   Harlem,
the south side of Chicago, the Detroit ghettos are created by
White America.   Black people are tired of talk--they want
to control their schools.

In order to maintain the status quo, boards of education have created another concept--decentralization.   Many
major cities are now headed toward decentralization.   Decentralization, however, is another fraudulent device to keep
"down" blacks and Puerto Ricans.   Under decentralization,
the people have no power, and hidden in the fine print are
the rules, regulations, and contractual obligations which in-
sure the continued supremacy of the old guard, inept racist
educators who have been responsible for the failure of the
schools to educate children.

Another area of discontent is reading and standardized

testing. For those who believe that reading is the biggest
problem in education today, I am going to suggest that this
simply is not so! I am not minimizing the importance of
reading. I am suggesting to you that it is only one of the
important factors in the quest for a decent life style. Even
if all black youngsters were able to read . . . then what?
Would it open doors for employment? Would it open housing
facilities? No! One of the basic problems in education today is that in itself, education cannot solve the social diseases which are destroying this country.

Standardized testing has been a household word in education for a long time. There have always been reasons
for the poor performance of black pupils on standardized
tests, a fact which Ocean Hill tried unsuccessfully to bring
to the attention of the Board of Education. Let me illustrate.
In one classroom in Ocean Hill there was one teacher for
the third grade. Right next door to that teacher was another
third grade teacher, but she had a paraprofessional working
with her. Two doors away there were two teachers and a
paraprofessional; and in the third class there were three
teachers. When all of those students are subjected to a
standardized test, the results do not reflect whether there
was one teacher, three teachers, or five teachers; nor does
it reflect how much experience the teachers have. You
simply subject youngsters to an evaluative instrument that
has no relevance.

After test results are tabulated on standardized ex-
aminations, a public relations job is done on the success and
failure of specific schools and their children. The question
which has been repeatedly asked of the professional staff is
that once you administer the standardized test, of what instructional value is it? In Ocean Hill there was an attempt
to bring together a group of professional people to assess
various instruments and construct new ones. A new instrument was eventually developed which was applied to approximately 4, 000 elementary school children. From several
sources, words of commendation were received about the
instrument. The instrument produced the kinds of data which
were relevant. Nevertheless, the Board of Education continued to request that we use outmoded standardized testing.

In the three years Ocean Hill was in operation, discipline problems declined, and there were no suspensions.
Does this mean that Ocean Hill did not have youngsters who
had problems? No, I don't say that; but they had other re-

sources to work with the students so that youngsters were
not penalized and stereotyped by suspension hearings. Regarding teacher absence in Ocean Hill, it went down approximately 16 percent; teacher turnover declined from 30 percent
to 1 percent; pupil attendance increased from 63 to 94 percent.

    Pupil attendance dramatically improved despite the
fact that Ocean Hill is in the heart of an urban renewal area
in which many buildings have been destroyed. In one particular area, 425 children were relocated, all of whom attended
the same elementary school. So the attendance for that particular school dropped and so did the district attendance
figures. The Board of Education in their naive way pointed
out that Ocean Hill had the worst attendance record in the
city; the Attendance Bureau was unable to locate these families. What actually happened was this: If they had dis-
charged those 425 children from the school register, we
would have lost teaching positions. So we kept them on our
registers, and we had an average of two teachers for every
classroom. As a result, the children in these classes pro-
fited greatly. This is an example of how local people can
manipulate the system once they find out how it works.

    What happened in Ocean Hill is exactly what is hap-
pening in Chicago, Detroit, and other urban areas. The
schools, the clientele, the parents and the children are demanding participation in educational affairs. Educators,
along with the mass-media, have for too long distorted the
demands of the people, especially the blacks. They made
community control and those who advocated it appear like
something frightening, a threat to us all. In fact, it is not.

    The price of education today is increasing rapidly;
but, I regret to say, there is no correlation between the
cost of education and the success of the process. In other
words, if big business, say, continued to process raw materials and the end product was as slipshod as the product
produced by public education, big business would go out of
business! But it seems that education just continues to roll
along.

    What I am trying to say is that, if we can put aside
issues such as teacher security, and look at what all the
emphasis should be on--educating children--then we find that
the concept of community control, sweeping through the
country, is probably the best thing that ever happened to

public education in this nation.

The sooner we begin to work towards restructuring education, the better off are our chances of saving this country. If we do not do it in the next few years, there is not going to be a country.   Now is the time to act!

4. SCHOOL COMMUNITY CONTROL
AS A SOCIAL MOVEMENT

by Preston Wilcox

The two people whom I will always accredit as having
initiated the first move in the history of this country for
community control of the schools were two black females--
E. Babette Edwards and Helen A. Testamark. My recollec-
tion is that they were the "green thumbs" who nurtured and
engineered the initial thrust for community control at Harlem's I. S. 201. They were and they still remain suspicious
of professional expertise and competence; they both have
steel trap minds capable of dealing with any school official
from Board of Education president to custodial staff; and
they are deeply committed to the education of minority group
children. As participant-theoreticians at that stage of the
struggle, it was their inability to be bought off or compro-
mised that convinced me of their commitment to build and
sustain a struggle.

Neither of these two teachers ever believed that the
New York City Board of Education ever had any intent or
capability to respond to minority group children as human
beings. Neither ever or even now believes that the vast
majority of teachers are willing to risk themselves on behalf
of their charges. Both still reject the language of oppression such as "culturally deprived," "disadvantaged" and all
the code language used by the Establishment to prevent calling minorities "nigger." "Inner city, " "newcomers, " "urban
crisis" are professional jargon for "nigger. " Helen and
Babette understood it all too well. Their ability to read this
racist system as it really is gave them a decided advantage.
They could not be managed by a bureaucratic system which
depended heavily on blind compliance to its irrelevant rules
and procedures for its continued existence.

Having been present on many of their encounters with
the Board of Education, state officials, Negro statesman, and
other public officials, I observed their consummate skill in
avoiding a response to the language of containment:

30

You cannot change an entire system by starting
with one school.
Don't you want a qualified principal instead of a
black principal?
Even though you disagree with McGeorge Bundy,
why don't you meet with him anyway?
We will support you if you agree to carry out
steps (1) and (2) as outlined by us.
Isn't that 'racism' in reverse?
If you get rid of Herman Ferguson, we will sup-
port you.
Who do you represent?

The question was not whether or not they wanted to
become a part of the system.   The question became how
could they alter the school system to make it work on behalf of minority group children.   When that question was
asked of a righteous person, one who did not have a need to
rationalize his own deprivation, there was but one alternative: to acquire the knowledge, skills and insights to subvert
the school system.   Importantly, these two activists recognized several basic truths:

a)   The materialistic "money on the mind" values of
this society propels superordinates to expend their energies
learning how to get subordinates to line up, how to "divide
and conquer" them, and how to get them to adjust peacefully
to an inhuman existence.
b)   The reality of white institutional racism had
rendered large numbers of white people incapable of making
humane decisions about the lives of minorities.
c)   Professionals had turned the school system into
an employment playground; an arena for earning tenure for
not doing the job they were being paid to perform.
d)   Parents had been conditioned to delegate the responsibility for educating their children to a school system
which systematically denied them a voice.
e)   Large city boards of education have never been
representative of the interests of the poor and of the minorities.
f)   The inhumanness of large school systems is a
prerequisite for its continued maintenance; it requires that
its consumers subscribe to the same inhuman values.

Given those truths, how can meaningful educational
change be achieved?   The requisites for change are based
on avoiding becoming a participant in the integration-segre-

gation argument since both arguments were designed to maintain white control over minority group education and to build a minority group constituency for the white agenda. This was achieved by substituting the stance of an articulate spokesman for that of an aggrieved complainant. When the I. S. 201 activists began to maintain that one could be black or Puerto Rican and successful, it unsettled the minds of their oppressors. Such actions rendered white liberalism unemployed and the anti-blackness of the overt racists ineffective. It is a myth that the beauty of blackness coincides with the antipathy which white racists hold for blackness. White racists hate blackness. The decision to perceive it as being beautiful was generated by blacks.

A second requisite for change is that of rejecting the pursuit of the values and the definitions of the oppressors. To do so would require that minorities utilize corporal punishment against their own kids and hate them as a way to win a response from the system. Recall that the services which are imported into minority group communities require a prior categorization of the ills and problems before appropriations are made. It is illegal to be black in this society. To be legitimized by the "system" is to be freed to produce drop-outs, drug addicts, criminals and the like.

A third requisite for change is to begin to learn how to behave toward black and Puerto Rican youth as though they counted just because they exist. To become their advocates and not their prosecutors is an important act in itself. To understand that their suffering is much more a factor of the system's negative definition of them than it is a factor of their own characters is also required. By any objective criteria, the system is stacked against them: it is organized to punish them, not reward them. This motive force has, perhaps, been the most propelling part of the movement. White America is slowly losing its ability to define minority group youth in a negative way in order to contain them. Such communities know now that they can survive. They are now opting for living, or for dying with honor.

A fourth requisite for change is that of incorporating an ability to sustain and endure crises. The uncertainty of life which was once a bane to the existence of oppressed minorities has now become an asset. Establishment types survive on order; oppressed peoples are masters at moving from crisis to crisis. Corollary to this phenomena is the development of a perception among minorities that they are

victims and are not powerless.   Those who define themselves
as being powerless by this definition bestow power upon those
in official positions.   Those who define themselves as victims have an overwhelming need to manage their own de-
victimization.   In the same way that Nixon has become a
victim of having achieved "the impossible dream, " the vic-
timized are learning how to succeed in guiding their own
self-resurrections.

A fifth requisite for change is to redefine the function
of the school and the concept of education.   Professional and
system control have been largely maintained by the act of
imposing their own definitions on the consumers.   Educational consumers in ghettos have sought to modify those definitions.   The problems of police brutality, deteriorated
housing, poor health, unemployment, inadequate welfare
allowances and drug addiction are increasingly being viewed
as educational problems.   Education is being perceived as a
political act.

> The white police system in such communities func-
> tions as "occupational troops" to protect outsiders
> from local residents.   The brutalization of minority
> group residents is endemic to its functioning.
>
> The drug traffic is deliberately concentrated within
> such communities.   It persists and expands because
> of police collusion.   It has been said that one is
> either a part of the problem or a part of the solution
> and even that the solution is a part of the problem.
> That's the way it is with the drug problem.   The high
> incidence of drug addiction is no accident.   In several
> recent incidents, police informers utilized drugs as a
> means to frame the targets of their interests.   Drug
> addiction is becoming a way to perpetuate genocide.
>
> The inadequacy of the welfare allowance produces a
> nutritional problem of broad dimensions.   Teachers
> as a group feel better about children who read.   Evi-
> dence suggests that they have little or no feeling
> about whether their children eat or not.   It took the
> Black Panther Party to highlight the need for break-
> fast programs in this country.   The Young Lords
> have picked it up.   As their young charges eat, they
> are also having their heads put in the right place.
>
> Housing conditions in such communities are both

illegal and inhumane. Teachers don't visit homes
largely because they will be confronted by their own
lack of caring when they do so. If they really cared
the classroom system would become a social action
system. The children would learn how to read the
impersonality of this society as a requisite for moti-
vating themselves.

The school community control movement cannot be
fully understood unless it is put into the context of the to-
tality of the black man's existence on white soil stolen from
the Indians. The enslavement of black people, the systematic denial of their rights, and their history of oppression
and subjugation have bestowed upon them a compelling need
to utilize their energies in confronting themselves as a
means of fostering their own liberation. The little red
school house was deliberately chosen as the site for the confrontation. The control of black minds by white America
has been its foremost skill of oppression. Secondly, it was
an arena where the political, the economic, the physical and
the social could be combined into a single whole. Importantly, it lent itself to involvement of the family, not just
the student, as a part of a community. The school was
actualized as the political instrument it has always been except that now it would become a laboratory for black liberation, rather than black containment.

This movement has been defined and generated by
minorities in this country. It is no accident in history that
it began in the poorest section of the best known ghetto in
the world. It is not an accident that an architectural pallia-
tive failed to anaesthetize the subject community. It is no
accident that the crisis has been sustained and the struggle
escalated. The struggle itself has been the foremost educator.

Minorities have learned once and for all that their
interests are vested in meaningful social change, not mere
upward mobility. They have learned that their linkages to
the Pan-African scene and to the Third World are deeply
embedded in their abilities to refuse to acquire the skills
and values that free them to oppress others. They have the
most to gain by creating a pluralistic society. They have
the most to gain from controlling and managing their own
destinies. Their skill in exercising power from a presumably powerless position is an additional asset.

Every black knows that white America does not believe that blacks will ever control their own schools. Whites
feel so self-assured because they know that they have the
biggest and most powerful weapons of destruction. It is a
fact that whites have "guns on their mind" and blacks know
it. What's more, whites have little compunction about turning their guns on their own. Witness Kent State and the
"generals" who head up institutions of higher education.
College presidents have become national guard "commanders"
even as their students have tried to rid their campuses of
the ROTC.

Blacks have learned that few whites have much interest in the disarming of other whites. They feel that
they need to keep their guns in reserve in the same way
that white liberals depend on white conservative support during crises and on the maintenance of white institutional
racism during stable periods to maintain their statuses. The
challenge for blacks, Chicanos, Indians and Puerto Ricans
has become that of liberating themselves without being forced
to pick up a gun and not precipitating its use by the white
system. The school community control movement provided
the first avenue for this approach.

This movement has exposed the "labor union" mentality of teacher associations in the Up South and in the
Down South. Any relationship between educational creativity
and teacher organizations is strictly accidental. The position
of the National Association for African American Education
is that black educators should give up membership within the
AFT and the NEA and begin to act and behave as advocates
for the students. This distaste for union membership is sure
to deepen within minority group communities and to be re-
placed by community unions designed to prevent fragmentation
and to achieve "operational unity." Parents, teachers, students and community will organize to create a single viable
political instrument. The increasing replacement of "interracial councils" in urban areas by black urban alliances is
another case in point.

The demise of the union movement within the black
community has been characterized by the growth in the number of all black teacher organizations and their alliance with
other community groups. This pattern has been escalated to
the national level by a growing number of national black organizations and national black caucuses within multi-racial
national organizations.

A second movement pattern is the growth of independent black educational institutions from pre-school through
college level. At least 20 such schools were to have held
their first national meeting in Los Angeles in August, 1970.
These schools fall into two categories: physically independent
and psychologically independent. Their common feature is
their advocacy on behalf of minority group students. A similar move toward the establishment of independent educational institutions is alive in the white community. There is
one difference: they are still toying with how to integrate.
Their minority group counterparts are targeting in on how-
to-educate for humanization.

A third pattern is the movement for control of police,
of hospitals, of health centers and of anaesthetizing opera-
tions like Model Colonies, Negro Removal and anti-depoverti-
zation programs. I suspect that the next major movement
will be that of controlling the prisons. Blacks are convinced that they can never be as cruel to their own as the
white man has been. It's just that simple.

A fourth pattern has been that of escalating the movement to a national level. At least 47 cities in this country
are engaged in finding new and more sophisticated ways of
deceiving black students and communities. They are offering
to "de-re-centralize" to mute the local struggles for community control. Afram's Action Library has a roster of 75
organizations from coast to coast which are actively advo-
cating community control and/or decentralization. At least
three states (New York, California and Pennsylvania) have
developed legislation leading to decentralization. The black
studies movement on college campuses is a direct response
to the school community control movement. Recall that
black students have not only demanded a humanization of the
curricula, they have also sought autonomy or a role in the
selection of the staff and in the recruitment and admission of
students. At Antioch College the students demanded black-
controlled dormitories as legitimate educational instruments.
The program was wiped out, not really because black students segregated themselves, but because they wanted to
control the content and nature of their own separation. This
movement, too, had its beginnings in the school community
control movement.

A fifth pattern is the development of a new body of
knowledge about education in general and black people specifically. Over 1000 articles have been published on the

subject, community control/decentralization, since the movement began.   A growing number of black scholars and white
humanists are putting together bodies of knowledge which
define the black condition in human terms.   There are at
least 12 centers of information about community control of
schools which did not exist before the confrontation at I. S.
201.

The thrust toward learning how to create human institutions has also been propelled by this movement.   New
roles for principals, students, teachers and parents are
being articulated, transmitted and carried out.   The theme
related to an effort to rid schools of their oppressive ex-
ploitative characteristics.   Efforts are being undertaken to
narrow the gap between the consumers and the producers
and to assign specific powers and responsibilites to all of
the actors.   New techniques of conflict resolution are being
developed and communities are developing the skills to solve
their own problems without the intervention of outsiders.
Recall that the black urban rebellions were cooled out by the
blacks themselves even though the guns of the National Guard
were on the scene.   Black people cared too much about each
other to send each other to slaughter at the hands of the
police.

The major dimension of the school community control
movement is the problem it has provided for white people.
White principals by the hundreds are being taught daily that
they too have been miseducated.   Most such principals now
spend their time locked up in their offices trying to avoid
being noticed.   Ill-equipped teachers are trying to find new
ways to explain their failures to teach.   They can no longer
complain of parental apathy when the school doors are being
knocked down by the parents.   They can no longer claim
that black students do not want to learn when such students
close down schools because teachers fail to teach them.
They can no longer claim superior intelligence, despite Jensen and Shockley, when their so-called superior intelligences
cannot be measured in terms of meaningful student achievement.   Their "liberalisms" are going wanting for takers.

The growing militancy of teacher organizations can be
said to be a direct consequence of the efforts at Ocean Hill-
Brownsville and I. S. 201 to involve parent/community leaders in the selection and evaluation of teachers and administrators.

Teachers are now more heavily involved in educational planning and community participation in the less chance areas of the nation. It is both a requisite for survival and an educational imperative. Recall that it was the groups at I. S. 201, Two Bridges and Ocean Hill-Brownsville who first considered that teachers be represented on policy-making boards.

Blacks are saying that the credential system, tenure as currently known, grades, IQ tests, admissions criteria and so on are like "Mason-Dixon" lines on the minds of whites. Such "standards" are utilized to exclude, not include; to control, not liberate; to discipline, not develop self-reliance; to line students up, not to help them not need a line.

A raft of administrative and teacher training programs have sprung up as a means to equip teachers to do their jobs. The thrust toward accountability in terms of performance, engineered by parent/community groups, has resulted in new learning opportunities for those who in the past insisted that failure was the fault of the families and their children. Teacher training institutions will never be the same - if they survive.

Interestingly enough, black communities need the resistance of the Establishment as a means to get themselves together. The Establishment demonstrates daily that it does not believe in the Constitution which it demands that minorities uphold. In addition, the thrust to control the schools within the black community is not perceived by blacks as an infringement upon white power. Rather, it is perceived as a non-negotiable expression of authentic black power. The control over institutions that serve one's community is a God-given right; the control over the internal relationships within one's community compounds this demand. Part of the confusion results from the differential perceptions of power and its uses. White communities struggle to gain the power to keep blacks out (neighborhood concept) and to be comfortably controlled by the system. Black communities are struggling not to be controlled by the system and to exclude no one. Part of the problem relates to the need of whites to control blacks as an end itself even if whites have to sacrifice their right to self-determination to do so.

Perhaps one of the most important learnings coming out of the movement is the recognition by a growing number of whites that their own salvation is inextricably tied to that

of the oppressed masses.   A crisis coalition that developed
during the height of the Ocean Hill-Brownsville conflict involved white radical students, Black Panthers, the Peace
and Freedom Party, the Freedom and Peace Party, CORE,
SNCC, the Republic of New Africa, the Black Caucus within
the UFT, a white coalition within the UFT, religious groups,
the NAACP, the Progressive Labor Party, the Urban League,
the Jewish Teachers for Community Control and the like.
Here was a group of organizations with divergent ideologies
coming together around a single issue.   Two groups were
missing: the white liberal establishment and their overt
racist bed partners.   The self-righteousness of the Up South
was exposed and later confirmed when Congress took action
to balance the racism of the Up South with that of the Down
South as it related to school desegregation.

     This shift in white awareness exposed the unions as
Down South liberals and Up South racists.   It turned white
liberalism into an Up South luxury and white conservatism
into an ally to black progress.   The silent majority is the
counterpart to the vocal black minority, now supplemented
by white youth groups.   The incipient violence of the hard
hats and the chicken-heartedness of white liberals have begun to teach this society what minorities have long understood.   The scourge of this country is the violence of white
people toward each other, not just toward blacks.   Blacks
now understand why white liberals have always cautioned
them against the use of violence.   White liberals understand
fully the strength of white violence.   It can kill you.

     The most powerful lesson learned and the essential
meaning of the movement is that minorities are saying
something about all education and the society in their efforts
to control their schools.   They are saying that their lives
are worth living and dying for.   They are saying that they
want to learn to be human.   They are saying that they are
not going to replicate the mistakes of whites and pass them
on to their offspring.   They are saying that they will learn
despite the schools.   They are saying that they know that
they can achieve against great odds.   They have survived
nearly 400 years of a systematic design to destroy them.
Involved black communities began to convince themselves of
their own worth.   They began to feel better about themselves
and their capabilities.   This turns out to be much more a
confirmation of a concealed reality than it is a discovery of
new information.

The major challenge of the community control movement is to that of developing the kind of changes in behavior,
philosophy, attitudes and perceptions that will persist over a
period of time. In the final analysis, it is a movement to
get individuals to confront their "I" institutions first, to
perceive themselves as being inseparable from their membership in a group and to learn to function in humane ways.
It has provided a growing number of theoreticians with the
impetus to replace scientific colonialism with scientific hu-
manism.   It has provided opportunities to learn how to educate children without punishing them.   It has provided an
opportunity to link the classroom to the real world; and to
remove the invisible wall between school and community.
Importantly it has made the toughest job in America--being
black--a compelling necessity to achieve the skills to accredit oneself and to be in control of one's own self-determination.

Remember, everybody is somebody.

Bibliography

Aronowitz, Stanley, "The Dialectics of Community Control,"
        in Social Policy, May/June, 1970; p. 47-51.

Baraka, Imamu Ameer (Leroi Jones), "A Black Value Sys-
        tem, " in Black Scholar, November, 1969; p. 54-60.

Berube, Maurice B. and Gittel, Marilyn.   Confrontation at
        Ocean Hill-Brownsville. New York: Praeger, 1969.

Covello, Leonard, Beagle, Simon and Bock, Leon, "The
        Community School in a Great Metropolis, " in Educa-
        tion for Better Living: The Role of the School in
        Community Improvement. Washington, D. C. ; U. S.
        Dept. of Health, Education and Welfare, 1957; p. 193-
        212.

Dunmore, Charlotte, comp. Poverty, Participation, Protest,
        Power and Black Americans: A Selected Bibliography
        for Use in Social Work Education. New York: Council
        of Social Work Education, 1970; 67 p.

Gittel, Marilyn and Hevesi, Alan G.   The Politics of Urban
        Education. New York: Prager, 1969.

Goldberg, Gertrude S., "I. S. 201: An Educational Land-
    mark, " in IRCD BULLETIN, Vol. II, No. 5 and
    Vol. III, No. 1, Winter, 1966-67; p. 1-9.

Hall, Robert. "An Open Letter to Black Educators: White
    Teaching Can't Motivate Our Children." New York;
    Afram Associates, Feb. 5, 1969; 2 p.

Hare, Nathan; Lynch, Acklyn; and Wilcox, Preston. "Black
    Power and Public Education." New York: National
    Association for African American Education, 1970;
    13 p.

I Ain't Playin' No More [a film]. Newton, Mass: Educational
    Development Center, 1970. (Also available through
    Afram Associates, Inc. 103 East 125th St., Harlem,
    N. Y. 10035.)

Kent, David B., Jr. Proceedings of the First National As-
    sociation of Afro-American Educators Conference.
    New York; the Association, August, 1968; 77 p.

Levin, Henry M., ed. Community Control of Schools.
    Washington, D. C.: Brookings Institution, 1970;
    309 p. + indices.

Mamis, Nancy and Wilcox, Preston. "Toward a Policy
    Guide and Handbook for Community Control/Decen-
    tralization." New York: Afram Associates, February
    25, 1970; 5 p. + Appendix.

Means, Fred E. "Teachers Unions: Yes--Poor Children:
    No." New York: Afram Associates, May, 1970; 9 p.

Melrod, Margot. "A Bibliography on Decentralization."
    Milwaukee: Institute of Governmental Affairs, Uni-
    versity of Wisconsin, 1970; 28 p.

Montgomery, M. Lee, ed. New Perspectives: Findings of
    a Five Day Black University. New York: National
    Association for African American Educators, April
    15, 1970; 125 p. + Introduction.

Nyerere, Julius K. "Education for Self-Reliance." Wash-
    ington, D. C.: Information Bulletin, Embassy of the
    United Republic of Tanzania, March, 1967; 34 p.

Rubinstein, Annette T. Schools Against Children: The Case
    for Community Control. New York: Monthly View
    Press, 1970; 293 p. + Notes on Contributors.

Seabrook, Luther, W. , "A New Experiment in Black Educa-
    tion, " in Social Policy, May/June, 1970; p. 61-63.

Sizemore, Barbara A. , "Separatism: A Reality Approach to
    Inclusion?" in Racial Crisis in American Education,
    ed. by Robert L. Green. Chicago: Follett Educ.
    Corp. , 1969; p. 249-279.

Spencer, David and Wilson, Charles E. "The Case for Com-
    munity Control #1. " New York: I. S. 201 Complex,
    1968; 27 p. (mimeo).

_____ and _____. "The Case for Community Con-
    trol #2. " New York: I. S. 201 Complex, December 1,
    1968; 14 p. (mimeo).

"Tricknology or Technology: White Teachers in the Black
    Community. " New York: Afram Associates, Inc. ,
    June 8, 1970; 4 p. (mimeo).

Walton, Sidney F. , Jr. The Black Curriculum: Developing
    a Program for Afro-American Studies. East Palo
    Alto, Calif. : Black Liberation Publishers, 1969.

_____. "Education for Humanization and Social Re-
    sponsibility. " Sausalito, Calif. : Martin Luther King,
    Jr. School, 1970; 32 p.

Wasserman, Miriam. The School Fix, N. Y. C. , U. S. A.
    New York: Outerbridge and Diensffrey, 1970; 524 p.
    + notes, Bibliography and Index.

Weinberg, Meyer, ed. W. E. B. DuBois: A Reader. New
    York: Harper & Row, 1970; 443 p. + Bibliography
    (chapters 5 and 8).

"What Is Community Control of Schools: A Citizen Fact
    Sheet". Pittsburgh: Training Center, Community
    Action Pittsburgh, Inc. , 1968; 9 p. (mimeo).

Wilcox, Preston, "The Community-Centered School," chapter IX in The Schoolhouse in the City. New York: Praeger, 1968.

_____. "The Community-Centered School," in Radical School Reform, ed. by Ronald and Beatrice Gross. New York: Simon and Schuster, 1969; p. 125-138.

_____. "The Crisis Over Who Shall Control the Schools: A Bibliography." New York: Afram Associates, Inc., December 27, 1968 (vol. I, no. I) (mimeo).

_____. "Decentralization: A Listing of Some Ideas." New York: Afram Associates, Inc., Oct. 5, 1968; 8 p. (mimeo).

_____. "Integration or Separatism: K-12," in Integrated Education: Race and Schools, no. 43, III:I, January-February, 1970; p. 23-33.

_____. "The Meaning of Community Control," in Foresight, 1:3, 1969; 12 p.

_____. "On the Way to School-Community Control: Some Observations." New York: Afram Associates, Inc., February 20, 1970; 4 p.

_____. "The Thrust Toward Community Control of the Schools in Black Communities," in Racial Crisis on American Education, ed. by Robert L. Green. Chicago: Follett Educ. Corp. 1969; p. 300-318.

Wilson, Charles E. "Guidelines and Expectations for Community Consultants." New York: Afram Associates, Inc., undated; 7 p. (mimeo).

_____. "Year One at 201," in Social Policy, May/ June, 1970; p. 10-17.

Wittcs, Glorianne and Simon, "A Study of Interracial Conflict: Researchers Study Factors Surrounding the Explosive Situation in Troubled High Schools," in American Education, June, 1970; p. 7-10.

5. THE FAILURE OF OUR SCHOOLS

by Percy E. Sutton

I must begin with the obvious: our educational system is failing. Schools are failing to teach, students are failing to learn. We are constantly presented with dismal statistics of below par reading and math scores, of high dropout rates, of almost illiterate high school graduates. In the past three or four years there have been numerous studies, books and essays documenting the monumental proportions of that failure. I would simply note that the cruelty of the failure of our schools has slapped most hard at our black and Puerto Rican children. The dropout rate for blacks and Puerto Ricans is astronomical. While precise data for New York schools are not available, 1967 figures indicate that there were 10,000 fewer Puerto Ricans enrolled in 12th grade than in 8th grade; and there were 11,000 fewer blacks enrolled in 12th grade than in 8th grade.

Of those who do make it through high school and graduate, only a little more than a fifth of the students in predominantly black and Puerto Rican schools earn an academic diploma, while more than half of the students in predominantly white schools earn an academic diploma. On the college level, things are not much better. Even with the City University's program of open admissions, blacks and Puerto Ricans--who constitute half of the total public school population in the city--made up only a quarter of the freshman class last year. Nationwide, less than 2 percent of the students in major state universities are black. In fact, in 1968 there were more foreign students in all American colleges and universities than there were American blacks!

But it is a mistake, and a very serious mistake, to assume that only black and Puerto Rican and other minority children are suffering under our present educational structure. Every ethnic group, every racial group, every income group, every child in every classroom in America is being destroyed by our school system. And I speak of destruction not metaphorically, but tangibly.

44

Our school system is training our children such that
they will be unable to cope with America of 1971, the America of their youth; and such that they will be unable to cope
with America of 1981 and 1991 and 2001, the America of
their adulthood. Our schools perpetuate a mythical, distorted and misleading view of ourselves and our society, an
illusion that results in powerlessness to control our own
lives and our own destinies. Our schools project a picture
of who own wealth, of who gets government subsidies, of who
controls the corporations and the communications media, of
how we go to war and why, of how government and politics
operate, of what our ghettos are and how they got that way--
a picture that is grotesquely out of focus with contemporary
realities. It is a picture with the widest and most cavernous
gaps. It is a picture that totally ignores the realities of the
corporate state, the military-industrial complex, the usurpa-
tion of legislative power by the administrative branch of
government, the fiscal and political obstacles to rebuilding
our cities, and the relationship between regulatory agencies
and the regulated industries, to name just a few glaring
omissions. It is a picture that makes it impossible to understand how to grasp the handles of power or even where to
find them. It is a picture that makes it impossible to understand the forces that are pushing and pulling at our lives,
and to harness and control these forces. It is a picture that
allows distant institutions and structures and groups of people
to dominate us. And it is a picture that makes the have-
nots unable to attack the root causes of their poverty and to
gain leverage in the power structure--for they don't know
what these root causes are and who or where the power
structure is. It is a picture that divides us, that makes the
have-nots fight the have-littles for the crumbs of power and
property. It makes us turn on one another and blame each
other--"it's those niggers, " or "those hippies, " or "those
construction workers, " or "those commies, " or "those Jews,"
or "those suburbanites. "

But despite continuous, six hour a day, five day a
week, nine month a year indoctrination by our schools for
12 straight years, our children are screaming "NO!" to this
picture of themselves and society. They are evolving a consciousness and a perception of their own that is incredibly
sophisticated and well-informed. Our children are increasingly articulating and acting out their skepticism of the entire
educational system and everything it teaches them. Some
would say that theirs is a nihilist and paranoid skepticism.
In the main, I think it is a justified mistrust. Our children

start out with the premise that the "big lie" is being shoved
down their throats not only by the schools, but by every institution and adult.   They assume that teachers lie, governments lie, politicians lie, parents lie.   And how did they
evolve this counter-view?   They evolved it not primarily from
reading Chairman Mao or Malcolm X.   They evolved it by
trusting their own senses and feelings and experiences.

They know ghetto life--they are told of American affluence.

They know their brothers and cousins return home
from a place called Vietnam in wooden boxes--they are told
of a fight for freedom.

They know that suburbia is inaccessible to the black
or brown-skinned--they are told of fair housing and freedom
of mobility.

They know of cops frisking, whipping out the gun, and
whisking off to jail--they are told of American justice.

They know the brilliant rock and jazz compositions--
they are told that only classical music is legitimate.

They know that Blacks participated in every aspect of
the founding and building of America--they are told that the
slaves picked cotton and sang gospels.

They know that the American Indians were the victims
of genocide--they are told the winning of the West was heroic.

The "big lie" is not just conveyed to our students
through the factual content of courses and textbooks.   It is
just as effectively propagandized through the structural form
of school itself.   Regimentation of class periods, fixed curriculum, repetitive indoor toil at uniform classroom assignments, strict behavioral discipline, dress regulations, sup-
pression of student publications and demonstrations, competitive grading, the tracking system, the "I-lecture-you-
answer" system--all these reflect a society that is neither
free nor democratic.   They reflect a society that is elitist,
racist, conformist, repressive, authoritarian, status conscious, middle-class oriented, male chauvinist and youth-
hating.   They reflect a society that is infused with attitudes
of intellectual snobbism, militarism, nationalism and capi-
talism.

Our schools stamp out all forms of curiosity, creativity, imagination, questioning, innovation and flexibility.
Our schools deny all opportunities to test, to search, to explore, to err.   They submerge individuality in a regiment of
groups, teams, classrooms and graduating classes where

uniformity, not diversity, is the ideal. The non-conformist
is the trouble-maker.

It is no accident that our school system has evolved
this way. Educational systems in any society perform the
function of socializing the young to adapt to their roles in
the adult economic and political structure. The basic elements that exist in 1971 American education were evolved
during the early and mid-20th century in the context of an
economy that was just becoming industrialized, bureaucratic
and metropolitan. In this type of society, the ability to in-
gest small bits of information, digest the right answers and
perform correctly on command were assets in the factory or
office. The intrusion of individuality, emotion, spontaneity,
joy, cooperation or questioning wouldn't get a person very
far on the assembly line or behind the desk. To climb the
ladder, you had to learn to keep your mouth shut and do what
you were told--you had to be the good organization man or
the good office housewife. But now our youth have begun to
revolt against being socialized to accept these roles, these
roles are changing--the entire social and economic structure
is changing. We are rapidly moving into a post-industrial
stage, when many low-skill white collar jobs are being eliminated by mechanization and computerization. The expanding
sector of the economy is services, both those of low sophis-
tication and skill and professional, technical and managerial
services. The fields of communications, research, the re-
tail trade and administration are booming.

The near future--the future of our children--will see
an even greater shift in the economy and the types of personnel needed. As science and technology vastly expand the
types of goods and services available as leisure time creates
new demands for new goods and services and experiences,
we will need new kinds of employees. We will need outer
space technicians, deep sea farmers, weather controllers,
ecologists, population controllers, genetic engineers, organ
transplanters, home environment designers. And as the poor
nations press more forcefully for the ideal of equal participation in the 20th and 21st centuries, we will need food production specialists, mass medical care technicians, module
home builders.

As the number of choices open to us expands, as the
number of people and cities and nations affected by new forms
of production and consumption rises, as technology becomes
more complex, and as trends such as urbanization and in-

dustrialization are speeded up, we will need quite a different
type of person to cope with society than that being produced
today by our educational system. We will need people with
skills very different from those of the 19th-century farmhand
or the early 20th-century assembly line worker or the mid-
20th-century file clerk. We will need people with broad visions of what can be done, humanistic visions of what ought
to be done, and realistic visions of how it should be done.
We will need people who are, in sum, future-oriented rather
than locked into the past.

     And how is our educational system preparing youth
for this world? History courses in public schools rarely
inch past World War II--that was a quarter of a century ago
to our children, although a living memory to many of us.
Urban studies are still a rarity. Black or Puerto Rican
studies are still debated as legitimate academic material.
Computers are beginning to be used, but other new technologies are unmentioned and unknown in the classroom. Thus,
even if our schools were not to fail, even if our schools
were indeed to succeed in teaching our students what they
propose to teach in the way they propose to teach it, our
schools would produce misfits. They would produce citizens
unable to assume the kinds of jobs and roles that their world
will demand of them.

     The existing educational system does jibe, however,
with our current system of political power and our current
consumption economy. Our educational system maintains the
distinction between those who rule and decide--the adminis-
tration--and those who follow orders docilely--the students.
Our educational system encourages the feeling that personal
worth is measured by external rewards, such as grades and
scholarship. This translates in later life into new Fords
and dishwashers.

     Thus far I have been concentrating my attention on
the public schools. Let me now consider higher education's
role in miseducating our youth and perpetuating the status quo.

     Despite all of the campus rebellion, all of the strikes
and protests, all of the rhetoric about reorganization of college rules and curriculum reform, all of the upheaval, our
colleges and universities still do little more than perpetuate
what our public schools have begun. The rigidity, the stul-
tification, and the conservative indoctrination are all there.
The artificial distinctions between specialties and fields, the

differentiation between learning from books, which gets academic credit, and learning from life, which is called "extra-
curricular activity, " are still there.   The glorification of the
trivial, the useless, the banal, and the archaic is still there.
The encouragement of competition and aggressiveness is still
there.

But a far more biting criticism may be made of higher
education.   If the goal of the public school historically was
to produce the minimal brain power to run the machines and
push the brooms; and if the goal of the high school historically was to produce the minimal brain power to run the
typewriters and answer the telephones; then the goal of the
university historically was to produce the minimal brain
power and the social contacts needed to plan and run the
economy and the government.   The captains of industry and
the captains of politics were trained for their roles in our
"institutions of higher learning. "   Thus our colleges and
universities socialized their students into their roles as
society's so-called leaders.

In order to do this, in order to teach the acquisition
and manipulation of economic and political power, the universities could only accept an elite into the ivory tower.   The
economic and political hierarchy could not afford too many
skilled competitors for the positions at the top.   It was
therefore not a regrettable accident, but to some minds the
correct thing that only a small social and intellectual strata
should be admitted to universities, and that the rest should
be left with the educational attainment appropriate to their
niche in the pyramid of power.   And so a system of higher
education has evolved that selects, and severely limits, its
admittants.   Our colleges and universities require an expenditure of time and money that only the wealthy or the
middle class can afford.   They require for admission a con-
stellation of personal attributes and social skills and cultural
familiarity that only those of particular economic and racial
origins have the opportunity to develop.   These requirements
have effectively filtered out the masses of people, and selected a small elite who have had access to the top of the
power structure.

Similarly, our public schools are structured so as to
make it difficult, if not impossible, for one who is not white
or middle class or male to get anywhere in the power structure.   Course content, educational techniques, and teachers'
attitudes are all geared toward a homogeneous population,

not an ethnically and racially and sexually diverse one. Our public schools thus practically ensure that certain groups won't make it through and thereby will have to drop out of the competition for economic and political power. I am not merely referring to competition for the highest rungs of power. I am talking about day-to-day survival, about jobs and political rights. Without a college degree, it's tough to get a decent roof over your head; but without a high school diploma, it's tough to eat. And so the tickets to a decent job with a decent salary--the diploma and the degree--aren't available to American minorities and women and poor whites. In this way, our educational system directly causes poverty and disenfranchisement in this country. Education is, as you can see, a bread-and-butter issue. Education controls access to economic and political power, from the highest to the lowest levels of power. It is true that today the old power relationships are crumbling and our educational system no longer so neatly funnels people into their once proper places in the power structure.

First, the middle-class intelligentsia, many of whom were educated in the city and state universities, have become the technocrats, the scientists and the professional consultants who are being absorbed into the upper echelons of power at the invitation of the captains of industry and government. Their expertise is needed, in fact required, for top level decision making and planning.

Secondly, whole groups of people in the underclass of society are seeking to take power. Blacks, Puerto Ricans, Mexican Americans, Indians, women and others are forcing their way into the power structure. They are demanding power through strikes, demonstrations, boycotts, sit-ins, court suits and other tactics; they are creating their own realms of power by setting up counter institutions--separate schools, newspapers, businesses.

Just as community activism and movements for community control and ethnic power have begun to change the governmental power structure, so consumerism and the ecology movement have begun to force the economic power structure to change. But despite these new forces of change, despite these new inroads into the power structure that bypass the traditional educational ladder, on the whole education still remains the primary mode of moving up in this society.

We come now to the toughest question of all: how can we change the educational system I have been criticizing? In other words, how can we open up the school doors and alter the school experiences?

One strategy is to seek to open up opportunities to higher education to those without money or a middle-class background. Pioneer programs such as SEEK, which I helped to found, or Open Admissions are steps in that direction. A second strategy is to vastly increase the input of money, personnel, school building, classrooms, and textbooks so as to concentrate more resources on each child. A third strategy is to equalize opportunity by desegregating schools, in terms of the composition of their students, faculty and administration.

But will these and other short-term strategies do the trick? Will they begin to make the fundamental changes needed in a system that is fundamentally off-base?

For example, will pouring money into the schools succeed in equalizing educational opportunity? With educational costs rising as astronomically as they have been, it has been estimated that $40 billion dollars more a year is needed to provide the kind of education now enjoyed by one-third of the population to the remaining two-thirds of the population. Forty billion dollars, whether from city or state or federal coffers, is a lot of bread. It's equivalent approximately to our expenditures on the Vietnam war. Is it worth it?

Thus far I have been referring to problems as they exist on a national, not global, scale. But as our spaceship earth grows ever smaller, we will have to think and act in terms of worldwide education. Is the current university structure or public school structure the least bit relevant to the masses of starving and homeless peoples in the underdeveloped nations? Should we spend trillions in aid to give them 30-seat classrooms and textbooks and tree-lined campuses? We have to step back and ask, what kind of education are we proposing to make accessible to all? If it is more of the same, it is worse than worthless, as I have indicated earlier.

In contrast to our present system, we need an educational structure that will deal with contemporary realities, such as the role of American enterprise in the economy of developing nations, the status of women, the cultural impact of the electronic media. I am not proposing that we replace Shakespeare with Franz Fanon and stop building colleges altogether. But we ought first to seek to radically diversify the kinds of experiences that qualify for academic credit and the kinds of places where education can be obtained. We need a form of higher education that trains us for life in the 20th and 21st centuries--for life as productive and fulfilled workers, as intelligent consumers, as masters not slaves of the new technologies, as participants in the new forms of family and social relationships, as decision makers. We need a form of higher education that functions as year-round, life-long skill and knowledge centers located not in one building or on one campus, but all around us in factories, in the home, in offices, in churches, in day-care centers, in shopping centers. We need schools run by not just one educational bureaucracy, but by a wide variety of groups and institutions--trade unions, corporations, parents, block associations. We need decentralized learning nodules employing as teachers skilled and knowledgeable persons from all walks of life--bankers, doctors, administrators, machinists. We need information exchanges where peers teach peers, and children teach children. We need a diversity of educational methods and courses that range from two weeks to two years in duration and from one specialized field to an entire subject in breadth. We need re-education programs that will retrain the unemployed worker or the employee who wants to switch occupations, that will update the mother whose children have grown up and who wants to enter the job market. We need to exploit the new technologies for education by using computers, satellites, cable television, holography, and data processors so as to create individualized classrooms in the home or car, so as to allow dialogue across many miles and many languages.

The effects of these sorts of changes in our concept of "education" will be revolutionary. Black people, Chicanos, plumbers, housewives, bus conductors, secretaries--everyone will have access to and the opportunity to obtain a "higher education" that is applicable to their own interests and their own needs. By drastically cutting down the cost of education and broadening the places where one can obtain it--in short, by bringing education to the people--we will begin to loosen up and then seize opportunities that have so long been clenched in the fists of the wealthy and the whites and the males of this nation. Speaking globally, we will begin to end the monopolization of opportunity by the Western developed nations. By setting up alternate structures of education with

different value systems, political outlooks and cultural view-
points, we will end the one-sided world view so long stamped
on the minds of our children.   By setting up educational net-
works that have feeders out into the real world, that interact
with institutions and events rather than merely books, we
will begin to discover what the sources of power are and
how power operates in our society; thereby shall we end the
ignorance that has kept us powerless.

There are some hopeful signs, some experiments in
these directions.   There is the new Medgar Evers College
in Brooklyn, whose classrooms are scattered throughout the
community.   There is the Open Classroom concept which
does away with fixed desks and fixed assignments.   There
are the street academies such as Harlem Prep which revives
the interest and enthusiasm of so-called dropouts.   There is
Sesame Street which uses television to educate pre-schoolers.
There is discussion of expanding the program of "external
degrees, " talk of trying an "educational voucher" system.
The experimentation must pick up drastically in speed and in
daring if we are to approach the kind of radical educational
overhaul needed.

As the demand rises in pitch and in force from the
underclass of this society--the demand for education in relevant subjects and in accessible forms--the walls of the ivory
tower will crack.   The bastions of scholars will fall.   The
privileged academics will lose their privileged places.   And
the people shall gain in knowledge, in skill, in ability, in
pride and in power.

It would be utopian to end on this note of optimism,
having begun on a note of pessimism.   But I am a politician,
and as such, an inveterate realist.   I know that even my
wildest dreams of educational reform will not create significant change unless there are concommitant changes in all of
the other institutions of society and the attitudes of its citizens.

I know that unless the prevailing trend of ever-in-
creasing educational requirements for jobs slows down, we
will be running after a train that we can never catch, re-
quiring post-doctoral degrees and post-post-doctoral degrees
for a garbageman's job.

I know that unless we attack race discrimination, it
will be true that a black man who completes college will

receive only 70 percent the income of a white college graduate; this is about the same income gap between blacks and
whites who have fewer than eight years of schooling.

I know that unless we end the war, we will never
have sufficient funds or resources to begin the most minimal
educational reform.

I know that unless we diversify ownership of the communications media, we will leave one of the most effective
and important educational tools in the hands of the white elite.

I know that unless we change our attitudes toward
women, the stereotype that professional education is unfemi-
nine will still prevail.

I know that unless we get our children out of the
ghetto, the best teacher or textbook or classroom will not
help our children learn who have a lead-poisoned brain and
an empty stomach.

Let us band together in the cause of educational reform.   But let us keep our horizons wide so that we set our
sights on the many other equally pivotal priorities for change
that challenge us.

6. THE TIGER WE DARE NOT DISMOUNT

by Carl Marburger

As an educator, it has been my hope to isolate some
of the problems facing urban schools--to remove and dis-
passionately examine them under a microscope the same way
a virologist might do, trying to find a cure for the common
cold. But urban school problems are not easily identifiable
germs that can be cured with separate injections--they are
intricately connected, interlocking parts of a whole. And
they cannot be addressed in a sterile, dispassionate environment.

In fact, when we speak of the urban problem, we are
really talking about the American problem. This nation continues to be more and more urbanized. The flight to the
suburbs is becoming--has become, in many places--merely
a flight to another part of the city; thus yesterday's suburb
has already become a part of today's urban complex. And
into this sprawling suburban environment begins to spill all
of the effluence of the cities--poisoned water, befouled air,
urban blight, urban greed, and urban ignorance.

The thought occurs that if this trend continues much
longer, the problem will have solved itself in another 20 or
30 years. By that time, we will either have been poisoned
or suffocated by our own neglect, or we will, like overpopu-
lated rats or lemmings, commit mass suicide, but in some
uniquely human way such as racial or class warfare.

I hope you will excuse me if I seem to be both passionate and cynical about the problem. Passionate, because
I believe that the ultimate hope for our way of life depends
to a large extent upon whether we are up to the task of saving our cities. If our great urban centers should suddenly
collapse from neglect or burn to a cinder in the fires of revolution, we would be finished as a nation. But, I still have
cause to hope that we can, indeed, save the cities. I still
hold the belief that most Americans do not want the cities to
fall and are willing to make many sacrifices to hold them
together. Nevertheless, I become cynical when I observe

how frequently our leaders in political life and in education
cannot translate this willingness into action, or when special
interests, greed or power politics are permitted to erode the
public's faith that practical solutions are desirable and
possible.

There are two ways of approaching the urban dilemma: One, we can merely choose to ignore the plight of the
cities. In this way we can bargain for time until the cancer
grows beyond the big city boundaries--by that time, it will
be someone else's mess. The second way is to tackle it
now--to save our urban centers while there is still something
worth saving--and in the process to save ourselves from our
own delusions about what is impossible. If we choose this
latter course, we must acknowledge that we are astride a
tiger we dare not dismount. We cannot approach the problem piecemeal; we cannot look at the components of the urban
dilemma--health, nutrition, housing, employment and educa-
tion--as separately curable diseases.

Now, I do not mean to imply that education is not an
integral part of the healing process. In fact, it may be the
most important component. But in saying that, we beg some
difficult questions about what education is doing, what it is
not doing, and what it is capable of doing to revitalize the
quality of urban life. I will address my remarks later on
to what I believe education is capable of doing. For the
moment, I wish to dwell on the question of what we are and
are not accomplishing. Both of these questions revolve, to
a great extent, around the matter of money.

When I stated earlier that the problems of the cities
and the suburbs are, in fact, a single problem, I meant that
these matters do not exist in isolation from each other. No-
where is the interlocking nature of our school problems more
apparent than in the matter of money. In most cases, the
underlying disparities between the cities and the suburbs are
not cultural or ethnic differences, but differences of wealth.
Even in our richest states, such as New York and New
Jersey, the wealth is unevenly divided between the cities and
the suburbs. The higher-income suburbs, with their healthy
local tax bases, are able to support their educational systems
adequately from local taxes alone; while the cities, with low
incomes, high density and deteriorating tax bases, are increasingly unable to maintain the same level of support.
Thus, there exists a wide gap separating the quality of education available to the children of suburban and urban schools.

The gap is widening every year.

It follows that if any substantial improvement in the educational programs of our cities is going to materialize, it must be accomplished by the wealthier districts sharing the burden of the economically poorer districts.   It would be a gross understatement to suggest that a voluntary share-the-wealth program between the cities and their surrounding suburbs is politically unfeasible.   Voluntary programs have been tried, and they have had some limited success, but these have involved the sharing of resources, not wealth.   It is quite clear that if tax equalization is to become an instrument for the revitalization of urban education, then such equalization must be stimulated at the state level.   Yet it is also quite clear that most legislatures, even those in typical urban states such as New York, Pennsylvania and New Jersey, are dominated by suburban interests, and tax reform in measure great enough to make a significant difference to the cities will not occur overnight.

What this means, then, is that the shortage of funds--a prime reason for the mounting crisis in education--can be expected to remain for an indefinite time.   It follows that if adequate funding is not forthcoming, some other method of changing and revitalizing our urban schools must be developed. At this point it is worth noting that even when large sums of money have become available, there has not always been a clear consensus on how it should be spent.   The goal is clear: the preparation of all of our children, regardless of race or socio-economic status, for participatory roles in society.   But the means to achieve that goal are far from certain within educational systems that still operate largely on a 19th-century model.

I wish to talk to you today about how we should change these systems to bring them into the 20th century.   First, we must know where change is possible.   I perceive it to be in four broad areas:

One--The teacher.
Two--The method.
Three--The administrator.
Four--The system itself.   That is, the political structure upon which we have built our schools.

In recounting these four areas, I wish to note an oversight.   I did not mention the urban students as an element

that can be changed. In other words, we cannot adapt the
student to the system (nor do I believe that to be the function
of education). We must change the system to accommodate
the student. This is what I believe we really mean when we
state the oft-repeated canto that education must be made relevant to the real world.

The Coleman Report made it abundantly clear that the
schools, regardless of how well they perform their traditional role, hold their pupils in loco parentis for a relatively
small part of their young lives. About 20 percent of the
total influence upon a child is exerted by the school. The
culture of poverty is a far stronger educational factor in the
life of the slum child. "The culture of poverty"--a neat
sociological term for squalor. I think the time has come to
forget euphemisms and take a hard, cold look at what it is
we face. When we speak of urban education and its problems, we are talking more and more about the education of
the poor American Negro. Each year the total population of
our cities falls and each year the Negro population in public
schools increases; each year the percentage of Negroes in
our cities climbs. Despite the efforts of local, state and
federal governments to change this pattern, the problem
grows worse. Urban renewal, more public housing, middle
income housing to lure the white middle class back--these
things haven't worked.

Let me cite some statistics from one ward in one
New Jersey city: Fifty-nine percent of the males are under
the age of 21. Seventy-two percent of the men above the age
of 25 have never finished high school. Forty-nine percent of
all residents come from five states--Georgia, the Carolinas,
Alabama, and Florida. These kinds of statistics exist in
areas of New York, Philadelphia, Chicago, Baltimore, Los
Angeles, Boston, and right on through the list of American
cities, large and small.

Thus, when we go about our daily duties of educating
the urban masses we are trying to educate the rural, southern poor, and now their children, in a northern, urban environment. We are trying to educate children with little
tradition of education. We are trying to teach them in aged,
neglected buildings. We are often using obsolete textbooks
and equipment. We are expected to send forth decent, in-
dustrious citizens imbued with the American ideal of equal
opportunity and the notion of a classless society. And we
are asked to do all this in a world where junkies and prosti-

tutes, street gangs and muggers, tenements and rats are
commonplace.

None of this we seem equipped to change. Yet, we
can change some things--the teacher, the administrator, our
methods and our system.

The teacher is the key person upon whom the educational system depends. His behavior and his attitudes, once
he closes the door to the classroom, determine whether learning, indifference to learning, or rejection of learning takes
place. The degree to which the critical process of socializa-
tion is accomplished is dependent upon his assumptions about
teaching, about himself as a teacher, and about children and
youth. Those perceptions become even more critical when
dealing with disadvantaged youth; those youth who often bring
to the classroom a value system widely at variance from
that of the teacher. If in the process of rejecting certain
values which are alien to his values he also rejects the child,
he reinforces the limitations already pressed upon that child
by his home and community.

There are two ways, I believe, in which we can remove the "curse" of this kind of teacher without removing
the teacher. First, there should be some method of reward-
ing superior accomplishment in the classroom. Merit systems and differentiated staffing are not new ideas, but they
are rarely tried in these days of strong labor unionism in
education. Especially in our urban schools, where rewards
for excellence can serve as a buffer against the frustrations
that teachers encounter, we need to look at some alternatives
to rigid pay scales, such as the establishment of associate
or master teacher levels above that of teacher. These levels
could be non-tenured, and the teacher could always revert
back to a tenured position. Basic to any of these premises
is my assumption that we must start out with a base pay that
rewards the teacher as a professional so that he does not
have to moonlight in order to provide for his family.

In the balance, however, I am convinced that tenure,
as an issue, is less vital than the preparation and certification of teachers. There is no logical reason why state
governments have permitted the proliferation of certification
requirements that have resulted in inadequate "gut" courses
at the teachers' colleges. The principle of certification has
real merit, in that it has been devised to maintain high professional standards, but over the years it has become so

rigid as to deny truly gifted college graduates the opportunity
to teach in the public schools. At the same time, because
it encourages mediocrity and traditionalism at the state college level, it produces an "official" teacher who is schooled
mostly in a form of pedagogy that is neither effective nor
relevant in the urban school. It is a sad but true commen-
tary on the miseducation of teachers that in New Jersey, for
instance, many majors in elementary education are required
to take more courses in the history of education than they are
in basic reading methodology.

It is of more than passing interest to note that most
New Jersey teachers agree on the inadequacy of their own
preparation. During a three-month period this year, the
New Jersey Education Association surveyed more than 22, 000
teachers for their attitudes about their training. A pervading
criticism was that education majors do not get enough training in the teaching of reading. The respondents also generally agreed that the colleges do not provide enough subject
matter preparation. Some of the other comments by these
teachers are revealing:

Said one, "There is no substitute for subject-matter
background as opposed to 'education' courses. "
Another: "Methods courses tend to be repetitious. "
And another: "Teachers should be required to visit
schools in the center ghetto areas and should do some of
their practice teaching there. They should be prepared to
reach the children who live there. "

What is most revealing is that the respondents generally agreed that teacher certification should be based on
proven performance rather than on completion of college
courses.

"A permanent certificate should be issued only after
the demonstration of a person's ability, " said one teacher.
Another remarked, "Just because one has completed
'X' number of courses is not a guarantee he can teach. Just
because a man graduates from law school does not mean he
can practice law. "

This survey indicates very strongly that teachers don't
necessarily want protectionism in the trade union sense. They
want better training and they want to be recognized for merit.
But frequently they are confounded in the attainment of these
goals by the rigidity of the structure in which they work and

by a lack of involvement in the administrative process. All
too often teachers are not made a part of educational decision making, nor are they permitted to inaugurate or devise
innovative practices in the classroom.

        This is where the administrator comes in. In indus-
try, it is middle management that provides the link between
the producer and the policy maker, the production line and
the executive suite. It is at this level that policy is related
to output. In a sense, this is the role of the school princi-
pal--he must translate educational policy which is determined
at the top level (the school board and superintendent) into
workable terms at the product level (the teacher and the student). But you and I know that it really doesn't work that
way. The analogy ends when you consider the nature of the
product. The school principal maintains control over very
few of the elements of industrial production. He cannot
choose his raw material; he has real difficulties redesigning
his production line; he cannot, in most cases, do anything
about inefficient production personnel; and he cannot guarantee the "product." In short, the school administrator is
a manager who cannot fully manage. There are a number of
reasons for this condition--most school administrators are
so caught up in shuffling papers and dealing with non-essen-
tial decisions that they are unable to perform true management functions. The administrator also must be, by the
nature of his "product," something of a political animal. He
must deal with the community in ways unknown to the industrial manager.

        Despite these differences, however, there is a dem-
onstrated need for the application of modern management
techniques to school administration. Most school supervisors
and administrators, having come up through the ranks, have
had little opportunity to engage in dialog with managers outside of the school structure or to learn modern management
tools and skills. Again, a large part of the problem lies at
the college level. Most graduate courses in school administration place disproportionate emphasis on curriculum and
supervision, with little attention being paid to management
training. Yet effective management systems and techniques
can be applied to virtually any problem besetting the urban
school administrator--labor negotiations, parent and student
confrontations, accountability and in-service training of staff,
application of new, more effective instructional techniques,
and modern planning methods. Moreover, proper training in
managerial skills can lead to better methods of identifying

and solving crucial problems.

It has been said that if Ford Motor Company used the management techniques current in many of our schools, the typical Ford car would cost $100, 000. That may be over-stating the case, but I believe we can utilize good manage-ment to examine and define some of the problems we have been encountering. As you know, there are a number of hypotheses that deal with this question of what we are failing to do in the urban schools.

First, there is the generally accepted idea that lan-guage difficulties, especially in urban ghettos, contribute to underachievement. We have been offering our educational resources to the urban child in our language, not his. Dif-ferent pronunciations, different meanings of words between teacher and pupil may be a significant barrier to effective communication. Second, we have some evidence that chil-dren learn better when they are permitted to learn at their own speed, rather than at a rate predetermined by the teacher's supposition of the student's capability. Third, learning environments that tend to distract students from structured learning retard their progress. Further, there is strong evidence to suggest that significant accomplishments can arise from applying individually prescribed instruction for disadvantaged children.

There are several other of these hypotheses. I don't believe it is necessary for me to read off a laundry list of them. But I do want to put some emphasis on a fourth factor, one I believe to be most important to the matter of equal educational opportunity in the cities, and one to which administrators and supervisors should apply the full weight of their influence and managerial skills. That factor is teacher characteristics and attitudes.

James Coleman has concluded that teacher attitudes and characteristics make a significant difference in the edu-cational achievement of disadvantaged children. He is not alone in this opinion. An ever-widening consensus of ob-servers and educators have been saying the same thing: the teacher can make the difference, if he is freed by the ad-ministrator. To make the urban schools function, we need the authentic kind of teacher--one who has sympathy and un-derstanding, yes, but one who also possesses a new kind of professionalism. By the same manner in which a teacher can destroy the motivation of children, he can also raise

expectations. It has been stated that behavior changes in a
child when his motivations change.   Put another way, an individual must want or need something in order to change.

In the view of New York State Regent Stephen Bailey,

> No greater responsibility falls upon the teacher of
> the disadvantaged than to change the self concept
> of those who enter the classroom feeling that they
> can never control the environment that surrounds
> them in their daily lives, and who lack the sense
> that knowledge and skills are the key to dignity,
> jobs and self-fulfillment.

Is this an impossible responsibility for the average urban
teacher to fulfill?   I know that it isn't.   But a large part of
the answer to that question lies in how the school administrator relates to what is going on in the classroom.   This
cannot be determined behind closed office doors; one cannot
appreciate why pupils learn from one teacher and not another
without actually observing performance in the classroom.
The administrator's role is crucial.

In recent years I have had an opportunity to talk with
many urban teachers who have experienced singular success
in raising the achievement levels of ghetto children.   In each
case, these teachers have told me that their success has
been because they gave children an opportunity to experience
for themselves that they can achieve.   The key to reaching
this level of expectations is involvement, with both the parent
and the community.   One of these teachers told me,

> Not too often do you have a principal who will
> allow you to innovate or experiment in a school.
> Both of my principals have been wonderful people.
> At times I thought they might say, 'stop, stop. '
> But they allowed me free rein to go as I desired
> to implement any idea I have which would get the
> little black ghetto children to read.

This teacher's remarks say a lot about what can be done to
improve the quality of education in urban schools.   But I
don't believe we should misinterpret his statement to imply
that all teachers have the same potential.

Again, the proper application of promising new ideas,
such as programmed learning, non-graded classrooms, flex-

ible scheduling, skill therapy and "free" schools, depends to
a large measure upon managerial skills--that is, the ability
to analyze needs, select techniques that work and to involve
the teachers in the design process.

I have here outlined a number of conditions which I
believe to be essential to change in the urban school environment.   I do not mean to suggest that these are the only elements.   There are many other promising techniques and concepts, such as combined community schools and day-care
centers, that should become parts of the picture.   Furthermore, we have strong evidence that early childhood nutrition
is an important factor in the achievement levels of poor
children, and we should be mounting a full-scale campaign to
extend pre-school services down to the toddler age.   But we
cannot look at this as a single approach or a panacea.   No
single solution can be viewed apart from all of the other solutions, some of which we already have in our hands.   What
we do not have is a comprehensive approach or a total commitment.

"If the school is to familiarize its pupils with the mainstream of American culture, " says Christopher Jencks, "it
must provide the slum child with an alternative to the self-
defeating style of his family and neighbors.   It must be a
home away from home. "   Granted.   But there is enormous
difficulty inherent in transforming the urban school into an
active agent of social change.   As Coleman has demonstrated,
20 percent is not very much time to work with.   Until we
can reach that other 80 percent of the child's life, we are
not going to make a difference in the ghetto.

Inasmuch as education cannot do the job itself, the
problem necessarily falls upon a much stronger arm of
government.   We can no longer afford to approach the problem of poverty on a fragmented and uncoordinated basis.   At
present, there is very little coordination of effort at the
higher levels of government.   Various agencies frequently
duplicate their services to the poor and dilute their own
efforts by interagency warfare over funds and programs.   It
is not uncommon in a large city to see health, anti-poverty,
welfare, social, educational and law enforcement agencies
each running identical programs and each performing inadequately because of lack of funds or carefully planned priorities.

I believe we must start thinking in terms of an urban

authority at the state or regional level that can effectively
coordinate programs and channel federal, state and local funds
into those areas where they will have maximum impact. (One
has only to examine the manner in which Title I funds are
now being allocated to recognize the need for a greater concentration of federal resources among fewer districts.   At
present, too much federal money is being wasted in small
towns and suburbs that really don't need it, on the theory
that there should be a piece of the action for everybody.)

I do not see such an authority as a threat to local control of education, but it would, of necessity, imply some
erosion of the power base of state educational establishments.
Such an agency would only be effective if it had broad responsibility to weld existing departments of state government
into a united force.   Acting under the ultimate control of the
governor, the authority would be empowered literally to order
amalgamation of existing agencies, to transfer agencies from
one jurisdiction to another and to abandon those bureaucracies
which no longer serve a desired end or which contribute to a
wasteful duplication of services.

It would also need the imprimatur of the President and
Congress, because many needed structural and funding reforms cannot succeed without the direct involvement of the
federal government.   Funds that are now dispersed among
various agencies through various federal offices stand a much
better chance of being directed to a common purpose when
the competitive factor is removed, and it can be removed
only through direct, authoritative action from the top.

This sounds like a threatening concept.   Indeed it is
to certain special interest bureaucracies.   But in fact, it is
not so much a change of power structure as a reordering of
priorities.   It does not change ultimate checks and balances,
but it does change who says what and to whom.   For this
reason, the President, Congress, the governors and the legislatures will need convincing that the urban authority approach
is an efficacious one.

At present, there is no nationwide coalition of forces
which could press for this kind of change.   The powerful education lobbies seem too busy fighting off the erosion of gains
already made, or they have been too busy pursuing support in
terms of dollars and cents, to seek a commitment for change
in basic governmental structures.

Yet the dire forecast of the Kerner Report--two Americas, black and white, separate and unequal--will certainly be fulfilled if we do not act quickly to change the urban environment. We desperately need a strong national coalition of educational, civil rights and political forces to revive pressure on federal and state administrations. We need more than a mere moral commitment. It must become a national goal rivaling the space program. Just as the space program cut across the entire fabric of government, so must our effort to revive our dying cities.

7. PAROCHIAL SCHOOLS IN THE INNER CITY

by Joseph P. Fitzpatrick, S. J.

In the place where I was giving some summer lectures
a few years ago, there was a delightful Jewish Rabbi who
used to amuse us constantly by telling us of Jewish folklore
and legends and stories.   And he told a little story of a
young Jewish boy who came to the Rabbi in great distress:
Master, he said, I am deeply troubled; here I am in my
fourteenth year, and it is not clear to me what the Lord is
calling me to be.   Ah, my son, answered the Rabbi, but it
is clear what the Lord wishes you to do.   Your father has
been a courageous soldier and your grandfather before him;
they defended your people bravely.   It is clear the Lord
wants you to be a soldier.   That cannot be, replied the boy;
for I was born of weak health, and my arms have not even
the strength to lift my father's sword.   Ah then, continued
the Rabbi, it is clear the Lord wants you to be a teacher.
Your father's brother was a renowned teacher, and your
grandfather's brother.   The Lord wishes you also to be a
teacher.   It cannot be, replied the boy, for I am slow of
speech, and my father's brother has tried to teach me the
Law, but I have no mind for it.   Then, replied the Rabbi,
it seems that the Lord is calling you to an impossible task;
in that case, it profits you nothing to consult the Rabbi; you
must go to the mountain and pray.

As I thought of our effort to try to define the role of
the parochial school in the inner city, I kept thinking of the
story of the Jewish boy.   The Lord has called us to an impossible task; it profits you nothing to consult the Rabbi; go
to the mountain and pray.

The problem of the role of the parochial school is
simply one more of the great ambiguities of our times.   If
we knew what education should be in the inner city (and I
think one would agree that we do not) and if we knew what
religion should be in the inner city (and I think one would
agree we do not), we would have little difficulty defining the
role of the parochial school.   But in a world where every-

thing is uncertain except uncertainty itself, it is no mystery
that the parochial school should be one more uncertainty
among the rest.

Be that as it may, there is one thing we can do; we
can examine the role the parochial school has consistently
played in the inner city; then we can ask ourselves, what is
the possibility that it could fulfill that role today? From a
purely sociological point of view, this examination is what I
would like to undertake.

There are certain obvious problems about parochial
schools with which we are all familiar. First the financial
one: as with all private educational enterprises on every
level, it is doubtful whether the parochial schools can fi-
nancially survive. Secondly, the whole character of religious
communities of sisters, brothers, and priests within the Catholic
Church is undergoing radical change. The numbers of religious personnel are dropping rapidly, and this decline of
religious personnel directly affects the ability of the schools
to continue. Finally, there is the serious question discussed
among Catholics whether the parochial school is any longer
a suitable institution to provide religious formation to the
young in a world like our own. So much for that. Let us
prescind for the moment from these massive problems. I
am simply presuming that despite these three very serious
problems the parochial school will continue. If it does continue, what is the role it can and ought to play in the inner
city?

I want to look at the role of the parochial school in
the lives of the poor immigrants who created it. Sociologically what did it do? It did two things: it preserved the
culture of the immigrants--their deepest values, the meanings of life which they cherished and which made sense in
their lives--and transmitted these values to their children.
Interwoven with those values, those meanings, that culture,
was their Catholic faith. It did a second thing: from this
basis of strength, it enabled the immigrants to move consistently and confidently into the mainstream of American
life. It was the basis of their identity, the focus of their
strength as an immigrant community, and the basis of their
political power which enabled them to make it in their adjustment to a new world. So, the parochial school preserved
for the immigrants the best of what they were and it served
as the transmission belt for them to move more fully into
American life.

I am not suggesting that this would not have taken place had the parochial school not existed. We can never answer that question. It is true that many other immigrants made it without the parochial school. In one way or other they were able to create charitable, social, business, and many other kinds of activities which served to give them a basis for identity and community strength. All I am saying is that, for large numbers of Catholic immigrants, this central institution was the parochial school. In fact, I have the impression that when Jewish immigrants and their children began to move in large numbers into the public school system, the public school in a Jewish neighborhood fulfilled for the Jewish people the same function the parochial school filled for the Catholic ones. It was in a profound sense "their institution."

This provision of a sense of identity to a community of newcomers was a secular function, although it so happened that the religious factor was central to the sense of identity and community strength. But emphatically it was a secular function being fulfilled by an educational institution under religious auspices. In all the evaluations of the parochial schools which I have read, the norms used to determine the effectiveness of the parochial schools have been religious ones: namely, did the schools turn out better Catholics? Were graduates of parochial schools formed in what we might call a "Catholic social philosophy," a sense of social or moral or ethical values which identified them as Catholics? The conclusions seem to be that on the basis of these norms of religious effectiveness, the graduates of parochial schools did not differ very much from the graduates of public schools or private secular schools. I do not mean to minimize the importance of these norms. But other things were taking place. A community which identified itself as Catholic was being given a sense of security in its traditions, a basis of self-confidence and competence by which they reinforced a sense of pride in themselves, and moved firmly toward adjustment to American life. Quite apart from adherence to a particular religious doctrine, or the practice of a particular religious devotion, or the acceptance of a particular Catholic social or ethical principle, the total life of the Catholic community was being rooted in American society. Historically and sociologically this was important. This apart, education proceeded reasonably enough in these schools.

Now to the central question: can the parochial school do it again, not with Irish or Italians or Germans or Polish,

but with blacks and Puerto Ricans in New York? Let me
take these up separately because they are separate issues--
the Puerto Ricans share a common Catholic faith with the
traditions of the parochial school and for the most part the
blacks do not.

Puerto Ricans

        Should the parochial school fulfill for the Puerto Ricans
the function it fulfilled for earlier immigrants? The answer
is necessarily "yes." Will it do this? It depends. If the
parochial schools--and by that I mean the Catholics responsible for the parochial schools--respond to the challenge in the
proper way, there is no reason that they do not have the capacity to do it. Whether we will do this is the crucial
question. It will depend upon three things: contact, culture,
and structure.

        Contact. This is a problem of numbers: how many
are we reaching? The picture is not encouraging and has
not been for years. In 1966, of all Puerto Rican children
who were in school in Manhattan and the Bronx, about 12
percent were in parochial schools. Last year it was about
15 percent--a steady but slow improvement. In the fall of
1969 there were about 21,000 Puerto Ricans in parochial
schools of Manhattan and the Bronx and about 120,000 in the
public schools of the same two boroughs. If the parochial
schools are going to be a basis of identity for Puerto Ricans,
they will have to reach more students. One out of six is not
enough, especially in the New York archdiocese. The officials of the archdiocese are reasonably convinced now that
more than 50 percent of all Catholics in the entire archdiocese
are Spanish-speaking, most of them Puerto Rican. That includes Westchester. If we wish to educate the future members of the New York archdiocese, there is no alternative:
we have to reach the Puerto Ricans. The Puerto Ricans are
a very young population, younger than any other group in the
city. The other Catholic ethnic groups are old populations.
There is no doubt where the future lies. If we want to be
with the future, we had better get with the Puerto Ricans.
And one in six is not being with it.

        I am not mentioning these figures in criticism of the
archdiocese or the parochial schools. Not at all. The archdiocese has done much for the Puerto Ricans: when the
story of that effort has been written it will be impressive.

But it is just not enough.   And I don't know exactly how to
make it enough.   Let me add a word of caution: figures are
tricky and they must be used with care.   In the inner city,
parochial schools are predominantly Puerto Rican.   For example in the parochial schools in those public school districts which qualify for Title I programs,   over 50 percent of
the total enrollment is Puerto Rican (15 percent is black).
In some cases,   the schools can't meet the demand.   What do
you do,   for example,   in Saint Cecelia's parish in East Harlem where there are over a thousand Puerto Ricans in two
parochial schools,   not one?   If the parish had accommoda-
tions,   it could probably fill a third school tomorrow.   Saint
Athanasius in Hunts Point outgrew the old school and the
parish built a new and bigger one;   85 percent of the enrollment is Puerto Rican.   Saint Joseph's in the East Tremont
area of the Bronx went from 6 percent Puerto Rican in 1955
to 66 percent ten years later.   In the inner city, therefore,
the picture is brighter.   But 85 percent of the Puerto Rican
pupils are out of contact with parochial schools in Manhattan
and the Bronx.   The first challenge,   therefore,   is numbers:
how do we reach them?

        Culture.   Contact is the first problem.   It is also the
easiest.   If we succeed in reaching the numbers of Puerto
Ricans whom we should reach,   can we understand them;   can
we bring them to understand us?   If we cannot,   the possibility of helping them achieve a sense of identity,   of community strength,   will be limited.   I cannot communicate with
a person unless I can explain to him what things mean to me;
but I cannot tell him what things mean to me until I know
what things mean to him.   This is the basis of intercultural
communication.   The same thing means different things to
people of different cultures: a deep sense of family loyalty
may prompt a Puerto Rican to favor a brother or a relative
over someone else competing for a job;   we might consider
the same thing a form of favoritism,   which we call corrup-
tion.   We are seeking to communicate our way of life to
Puerto Ricans.   We may not always realize that the way of
life we are asking them to accept may appear to them to be
strange,   inhuman,   sometimes even immoral.   Therefore,
unless we are sensitive to what things mean to them,   we
cannot have an understanding and a sympathy for their style
of life,   their interests,   and the things they cherish.

        Unless they sense this understanding in our minds and
hearts,   the Puerto Ricans will not be responsive to us.   If
they do sense it,   their reaction will be favorable;   they will

realize that we have respeto, for the dignidad which they are
conscious of having within them. From that realization
flows simpatia; we are on the same wavelength. With this
relationship, a sense of dignity, self-confidence, and identity
has a chance to emerge strongly.

Together with this sensitivity to the culture of the
Puerto Ricans, we must develop a capacity to create an environment in which the Puerto Ricans feel at home--en su
casa as they say--in which they are conscious of who they
are, of the background from which they have come, and of
the importance of the values they have brought with them.
It is not enough simply to introduce a course or a program
of courses in Puerto Rican studies. I think Puerto Rican
studies programs are important and I encourage them; but I
am always afraid that we may think we have completed the
task when the program is established. Courses in Puerto
Rican studies are no better than the professors who teach
them; they can become as deadening as courses of studies
in any other area. What is more important, indeed what is
essential even to a course in Puerto Rican studies, is an
awareness of the culture of the Puerto Rican people that
shows itself spontaneously in a casual remark, a tone of
voice, an off-hand reaction to a situation.

In the experience of earlier immigrants this was what
they found in the parochial school. The discipline may have
been severe, authority vigorously exercised, but they were
in an environment which made sense to them, in which they
were conscious of a basic respect and acceptance of their
lives and of what they were. This same kind of environment
will be necessary if the parochial schools are to do for the
newcomers what it did for the immigrants of previous
decades.

In my experience with the parochial schools, I am
convinced that this is the area in which the great inadequacy
is to be found, although efforts have been made to prepare
parochial school personnel for this intercultural understanding. The Institute of Intercultural Communication at the
Catholic University in Ponce, Puerto Rico, has just completed its fourteenth year. This is a two-month summer
program for priests, sisters, brothers, and lay persons who
work with Puerto Ricans on the Mainland. It consists of
basic language training in Spanish and courses in the background of Puerto Rican people, together with a living experience in Puerto Rican environments. Hundreds of teachers

from the parochial schools have been trained at this Institute and it has made a significant difference in the response of these people to the Puerto Ricans in New York.   But in spite of that, much remains to be accomplished in order to create an environment in which the Puerto Rican is at home.

Structure.   This brings us to the last of the three. If we can reach the Puerto Ricans in sufficient numbers; if we can arrive at mutual understanding; does the structure of our educational system permit us effectively to educate them? This is not only our problem; it is the problem of every school system in the nation.   And it goes far beyond the nation.   At two conferences I attended during the summer, one in Mexico and one in Puerto Rico, about the education of people in underdeveloped countries, the question was seriously raised whether conventional methods can possibly be effective in educating the millions of children in developing nations.   The same question is also asked of ourselves.   The ramifications of this problem are almost endless.   They range from questions on the highest level of educational philosophy to simple questions about the method of teaching reading or arithmetic.   They are not going to be settled by a talk at a Friday morning institute or a workshop or a semester seminar.   They will be settled by a long-term revolution in educational theory and method.

The part of the revolution that is available to us is this: the simple principle, so easy to say, so difficult to do, that we must adjust the structure of our schools and of our lives to fit the needs of the poor; we cannot expect them to organize their lives and their needs to fit into our structure.   I cannot spell out a blueprint for this.   Whether it consists in "happenings" like many of the activities in summer in the city, or programs like those of Monsignor Fox's Institute for Human Development, or Montessori methods, or the humble but human experiments of the little sister in grade 3 that never get written up in the educational journals or talked about at educational workshops, the thrust is in the same direction--to escape from the rigidities that we are not conscious of but which centuries of middle-class striving have built into our culture.

One aspect of the youth revolt is just this: they are trying to tell us in aggravating and bizarre ways that they don't want their importance as persons to depend on the grades they get in school, or the number of their academic

degrees, or the level of their occupation, or the size of
their income, or the address where they live, or the clothes
they wear. They want their importance as a person to depend wholly on their (sometimes literally) naked selves. I
have my complaints as I am sure many do about some aspects of the youth culture, but they are a modern voice
crying strangely in the wilderness to call our attention to
much of the artificiality built into our middle-class life.
Whatever else may be happening today, we are certainly
witnessing a massive movement in the world away from systems in which persons are formed by institutional processes
and toward systems in which persons work within flexible
structures so that they may form themselves. This is not
simply a question of struggling like the woman in Up the
Down Staircase until you prevail against a ludicrous bureaucracy that makes it impossible to teach. The modern trend
questions the very basics of the educational procedures that
had meaning for that attractive heroine.

        If we are searching for a meaningful role for paro-
chial schools to play, the role of innovation, experimentation, or courageous adaptation is waiting for us. As a
private system, the parochial schools should have a flexibility that no public system can ever have. And, in terms
of personnel, the religious life of nuns or priests or brothers
ideally should free them from the preoccupations which hinder
lay people. But we have never exploited these possibilities.
We allowed our school system to become terribly routinized,
tradition-bound and often just static. We were not alone in
this. Practically every school system has done the same.
And we religious personnel often barricaded ourselves behind
cloistered walls from any dynamic relationship with the real
world at our doorstep. Thank God, these structures are
being radically shaken. Perhaps now is the time that the
capacity for flexibility can be effectively exploited. If we
can generate the power to experiment, and the courage and
the vision to innovate, what couldn't we do for the minorities
in New York City? I was speaking some time ago to a
prominent educator who after years in the public system
joined the Fordham faculty. I asked him how things were
going. He answered with a smile: "This is wonderful.
Why, at Fordham I can do things in two weeks that it would
have taken two years to do in a public university."

        Therefore, with reference to structure, let me con-
clude. The entire educational enterprise, both public and
private, is going to be subjected to radical challenges in the

next ten years.   This is so because education cannot be taken
lightly in our generation.   It is the central and crucial issue
of our society.   What the nation and the world need is imag-
inative innovation; courageous experimentation.   If only we
can succeed in using it, we have the flexibility that no public
system has and we have a resource of mobile personnel that
no public system enjoys.   If we could make it work, we
might develop the models that could plot the path to the future.   How to do it?   Despite what the hippies say, it takes
a great deal more than love.   Let us never forget the amus-
ing but striking lesson in one of the "Peanuts" comic strips.
Good Old Charlie Brown is walking in great dejection off the
ballfield muttering to his equally dejected team: "Golly!
130 to 1! How can you lose when you're so sincere?" Good
will alone will not prevail.   It will require tremendous intellectual effort; the use of every bit of skill and competence
we can lay our hands on; humility and respect in working
seriously at secular tasks with secular experts; and a dedi-
cation to the service of the Lord which drives us to a dedicated service of our fellow men.

        Can the parochial school in the inner city do for the
Puerto Ricans what it did for earlier immigrant groups? If
it can succeed in contacting more of them, making the necessary cultural adjustments, and modifying our educational
structures, it may be able to do it.   If it can fulfill this
role, of providing a basis of identity and community strength
for the newcomers, this alone would be sufficient reason to
retain the parochial school.   Isn't this largely a "secular"
function?   Indeed, it is, but the fulfillment of secular functions is a perfectly suitable objective for people who are mo-
tivated by religious teachings or principles.   Nothing is more
"secular" than feeding the hungry; but we know this is a
function which is required by the teachings of all great re-
ligions.

The Blacks

        Can the parochial school do for the blacks what it did
for immigrants earlier?   Quite apart from the question
whether the parochial school can or ought to continue its response to the needs of the black community is the most serious challenge it must face in the inner city.   In terms of
contact, in the fall of 1969 ten percent of all students in
parochial schools of the New York archdiocese were black.
This includes all the schools of Westchester and the upper

counties.   From many points of view this is fairly impressive.   The parochial schools are doing much better propor-
tionately with the blacks than they are doing with the Puerto
Ricans.   In the poverty areas which qualify for Title I funds,
16 percent of all students in parochial schools were black.
As I indicated before, contact with Puerto Ricans in the
Title I areas is rather good, about 50 percent.

The serious charge of the schools in relation to the
blacks is twofold.   First is the challenge that the black community is raising against anything controlled by whites, including schools, demonstrating their reluctance to become
part of any system which is not clearly identified as black
and under black control.   If this issue could be resolved to
the satisfaction of the blacks, there is the further challenge
of adapting a Catholic parochial school system to a black
population predominantly Protestant.   The parochial schools
have never faced this kind of an issue before; but it is the
crucial issue of the inner city.

In order to meet it, the same three conditions would
have to be met successfully which I have mentioned in relation to the Puerto Ricans, namely: contact: the schools
would have to be able to bring many more black students into
the schools than are there now; culture: they would have to
create a cultural climate in which black students would feel
at home and would have a sense that the school was "their"
school in the same way immigrants felt about it generations
ago; and finally, structure: the schools would have to be able
to adapt their administration and curriculum, in fact their
whole style, to the needs of the black students.

Can they do it?   I do not know.   If they do not succeed in doing it, then I think we can add a fourth item--
economics--to the three major problems affecting the survival of the parochial school.   Can they survive economically;
will the decreasing numbers of members of religious communities make it impossible for them to continue; will Catholics decide that the school is no longer a suitable institution
for the religious formation of youth; and have they found it
impossible to adjust to the challenge of the education of black
students in the inner city by providing a basis for identity
and community strength?   I directed many of my remarks to
the role of the parochial schools with the Puerto Ricans;
that is important.   But the crucial issue of the inner city is
the black issue.   If the schools succeed in broadening and
improving the education of Puerto Ricans, but fail in expand-

ing education of the Blacks, I am afraid that partial success will be cancelled by major failure.

What is needed is imaginativeness, innovation, adaptation. If the parochial schools can meet the challenge, if the black citizens can be accepted into the parochial school enterprise, the schools could become the basis of a form of black power which would be similar to the power immigrants found in the institutions which they looked upon as "theirs" two or three generations ago.

What I have presented is an ideal. If the parochial schools survive, the role of educating blacks is one they could and should fulfill. Let me conclude with a few summary statements: It is important for a parochial school system to exist, simply as an alternative system, providing a range of selection to citizens. It gives them greater freedom, selectivity, choice; it relieves the obligatory character of a single system.

The choosing of this alternative system should not be based on fear. Unfortunately, this is too often the case at the present time. Too many parents seek the parochial schools for their children because they are afraid of the public schools, especially on the junior high and high school levels. Choice should be based on free selection. One reason for this selection could very well be the possibility of Puerto Ricans' or blacks' being able to find parochial schools more helpful as a basis of community strength.

Furthermore, choice of this alternative should not be resisted because of vested financial interests in the public school. Some years ago complaints were raised against parochial schools because, it was charged, they were divisive. Now, however, the complaint begins to shift. In the presence of a very real possibility of increased aid to parochial schools or parochial school students, the fear is expressed that this might drain off funds which should be applied to the maintenance of the public school systems. If the personnel in both the parochial and the public school systems could disentangle themselves from the controversies of the past and recognize the potential value of cooperative programs in alternative school systems, there is no limit to what they might accomplish.

A second point is that the parochial school system has some strategic advantages, if they could be effectively

exploited. The schools are there in the middle of the inner
city neighborhoods. The religious personnel who teach in
the schools generally live in the midst of the area. They
belong to it and if they can shake loose from traditional isolation (which many of them are succeeding in doing), they
are fellow residents, neighbors day and night, who should be
able to establish an identity with the neighborhood residents
more easily than teachers who commute into the area every
day.

Furthermore, they have the flexibility and adaptability
which a public system cannot have, if only the parochial
schools will use it. They have the basis for community control in the palm of their hand; they are ideally set up to
move it into a reality.

Third, it would be helpful if we had time to elaborate
ideas about the parochial school making social and cultural
adjustments to the inner city experience. The strength and
stability of newcomers to the city depend on their ability to
create a range of intermediate institutions through which they
begin to control their own lives and gradually come to manage the services coming to them from the large and complicated bureaucracy of the city. The school is one of the
most central of these institutions. Therefore, the involvement of Puerto Ricans and blacks in an educational experience which helps to give them a sense of identity and
strength is one of the surest ways to enable them to move
from this position of strength into the mainstream of American society.

8. A RELEVANT EDUCATION FOR THE 70's

by James Farmer

Because I have selected the theme "A Relevant Education for the 70's," it gives the impression that I have a blueprint for education in this decade. Actually, I do not have a blueprint and I cannot present answers to all of the questions of education in the decade of the 70's. I used to know the answers in the early part of the 1960's. Now I am not even certain that I know the questions. I do know one thing with certainty; the answers are not as simple as they once appeared to be. They are very complex indeed. The questions are changing just as the answers obviously are changing, and if one wishes to keep up with the intellectual and pragmatic requirements of our day, then he must continue studying, working, planning, and contemplating.

If an educator is to be at all effective in his profession, he must be familiar with the agenda changes that are taking place within the society. And there are many changes occuring. Recently, I received a call from an old friend of mine whom I had not seen for some time. He said, "Jim, I'm totally confused." I said, "What's the problem?" He said:

> You know, a few years ago you so-called civil rights leaders told us that the most meaningful thing that we could do was to integrate an all-white suburb. Well, we took you at your word. My wife and I bought the split level house in Lovely Lane, next door to Gorgeous Garden. We mowed the lawn, and took all of the gaff, rocks, sticks and isolation and now we have overcome. We are accepted by our neighbors. They invite us over for cocktails and we have them over for tea. But, now we are called Uncle Toms for living out there with all those white folks.

This was an indication of the change in the agenda. It was not long after that I was out in Los Angeles conduct-

ing a seminar for the Board of Education. In the course of
one discussion, some of the officials of the board informed
me that very shortly they were going to issue a complete
plan for the elimination of de facto school segregation. They
were going to wipe it out in one fell swoop. My mind then
drifted back a few years when I had demanded that the Los
Angeles Board of Education do something about de facto segregation. At that time, they did not even acknowledge they
had a problem. They said this must be a case of mistaken
identity. "You must think this is Mississippi. This is California. We don't have any segregation here." A few years
later, they said: "Yes, we do have segregation but it is de
facto and not de jure. Therefore, it's outside of jurisdiction, because we are the education authority and not the
housing authority." At a later date the Board acknowledged
that it was their responsibility but they didn't know what to
do about it. Now they had a plan which would wipe out segregation. Well, I had to tell them with a mixture of some
sadness and some amusement, that when they came out with
this plan, and if it is all that they say it's going to be, they
must expect that it will receive a lukewarm reception and
that in certain minority communities it would be met with
outright hostility because the agenda has changed so greatly.

Blacks today are not concerned with whether the black
child sits next to the white child in school. Rather, they
are concerned more with the quality of education which their
children are receiving. One reason for this fact is that we
have failed to integrate American society. There is less integration today than there was a decade ago or even at the
time of the Supreme Court decision in 1954. There is more
residential segregation now. Blacks do not see integration
as an avenue open to them. Our cities are becoming black
cores in white nooses with the inner city more and more
black and the suburbs increasingly white. This housing pattern, of course, promotes increased de facto school segregation. That is why there is more segregation in our
country's schools today than there was prior to 1954.

Many Southern cities are now following the example
of Northern cities by trying to substitute de facto segregation
for de jure segregation. The North created de facto segregation and maintained it. Southern cities are now asking,
"How is it that those Yankees," and they put the usual ad-
jective in front of the word, of course, "have managed to
maintain segregation all these years without anybody charging
them with violating the 1954 Supreme Court decision." They

found the answer in de facto rather than de jure segregation.
Now, Southern cities are following suit.   Urban renewal,
freeway construction, and new thoroughfares are devices to
uproot those residential communities which had originally
been integrated.

It must be remembered that in the South there had
been far more numerous integrated residential communities
than in the North.   But if the present pattern continues, in
a few years, Southern cities will be saying what the Northern
cities have said all along: "We have no segregation here.
Why anyone who lives in this school district is perfectly free
to go to this school.   It is an accident that they are all
white, or all black. "   Thus, we have not really created an
open society in our country.   That is another reason for the
changing agenda.

If there is any profession within our society which I
do not envy it is the education profession.   Educators have
the most difficult job in the nation.   The schools are the
front line trenches now, just as surely as the picket lines,
the jails and the marches in the deep South were the trenches
in the early 1960's.   In the 1970's I think the trenches will
continue to be the schools.   As I talk to parents, be they
black, Chicano, Puerto Rican or poor white, they are more
concerned with the quality of the education their children are
receiving now than ever before.   There was a time when
black parents, Puerto Rican parents, and Chicano parents
were a little stand-offish from the schools because the
schools represented not the establishment as much as officialdom.   And officialdom was terrifying because it had ultimate power over them.   Those blacks who had come from
the South had been afraid of officialdom because officialdom
could by decree cut them off welfare, deny them a loan, or
even chase them out of town.   There was a hesitation to sign
one's name to anything because one never knew what that
signature would be used for and when it would rise to haunt
the signer.   The schools represented officialdom and people
were afraid of it.   But now they have overcome that fear.
Because black parents know only too well that unless their
children are better educated than they were, their children
will find themselves handicapped in later life.   Poverty,
illiteracy and ignorance are selfperpetuating.   And so the
heat is on educators.

I do not need to elaborate upon the cliche that educators have not done their job.   When I say this, I am not

attacking the schools or their teachers.   The criticism is
aimed at society, myself included.   We have not been sufficiently effective in orienting our school systems to the task
of educating the poor, the non-white, blacks, browns, reds,
and those whose backgrounds are rural rather than urban.
We have not learned yet how to accomplish this.   Our educational system continues to be oriented toward the white
middle class, and it is debatable how well we educate even
middle-class children.   Clearly, however, we do it infinitely
better than we educate the black, the Puerto Rican and other
children who are poor.

        It is true, of course, that children who come from
families that are poor have many obstacles to the learning
process, such as the absence of books in the home, and
parents who cannot help them with their school work.   But I
would insist that it is a cop out to put the blame for our
failures on the parents, the environment or the community.
School men must share that blame because they must be held
accountable for their product.   I know that accountability is
a touchy point, but I believe with all the passion I can
muster that we must be held accountable for our products.
I get fed up with hearing teachers who say "Mr. Farmer, I
know I'm a good teacher, I got straight A's in education
while in college, so I know I can teach.   I know I am a
great teacher.   If my kids don't learn, it's their problem.
Something is wrong with their parents, their family, their
environment, or their community.   But I am a good teacher."
I would deny that such a person is a good teacher.   I think
that teacher is an impossible teacher.   If the children don't
learn, the teacher must assume a share of the responsibility
for it.   This may be unfair but I see no alternative.   In
athletics we hold a coach accountable.   If his team loses, he
is fired.   But in education if the class fails we put the blame
on the class, and not on the teacher.   I think we must reverse it now and hold teachers accountable.

        That is why I am in favor of the Clark plan in Wash-
ington.   I think that it would be more effective if it provided
in-service training for teachers so that they could be trained
now to teach children how to read.   It is astonishing that
with the technical knowledge available to us we can't teach
children to read.   In 1965-1966 I tried unsuccessfully to get
a national literacy program started.   But there was not sufficient interest in my plan.   At that time it was assumed
that if there were Americans who could not read that they
must be immigrants who did not know the English language,

but if they were taught the language, the problem would be
solved. Nothing could have been further from the truth. Today, there are 20 to 30 million adult Americans who are
functionally illiterate. We produce high school graduates
who are reading at a third-, fourth-, and fifth-grade level.
We have enough knowledge to prevent this. All we need is
the will to prevent this tragedy.

In large measure the responsibility for this situation
must rest with the teachers. Many educators say, "Yes, I
know children are not reading but give us more money and
then we can do that job. " It is true that there is not enough
money available for education. I want to see much more
money available for education, but not just to do the same
old things that have failed. For this will not accomplish the
desired ends. For example, I once observed an adult reading class in which a 250-pound truck driver wrestled with a
sentence about a visit to grandma's farm. This sentence had
no relevance to his experience. What I would suggest is that
we must seek to orient our teaching techniques and our materials to the needs of those who are rapidly becoming a
majority in city school systems--the non-white and the poor.

We must change materials. We must change the
teaching techniques. Standardized tests have a built in cultural bias. Twelve years ago a white psychologist devised a
test which had an opposite bias. His test had a pro-black,
Puerto Rican, lower-class and rural bias. But he insisted
that his test was no more biased than other tests and that he
would stake his professional reputation upon his conviction
that his test was as valid as those currently in use. He then
proceeded to administer his test to blacks, Puerto Ricans and
white children. The black and Puerto Rican children out-
scored the white children. Does that mean they were brighter? No, it just means that the test was biased in their
favor. Now if Jensen had observed such test results he
would have concluded that blacks and Puerto Ricans were
more intelligent than whites because their genes were superior. What nonsense!

Another test that is currently used in some first-grade
classes had a question which depicts three men--one man
wearing a tuxedo, one with work clothes, a third with a business suit. Children are asked which of these pictures was
a father going to work. According to this test, the correct
answer was the man in the business suit. Well you can see
immediately what that does to the child whose father was a

factory worker. A poor child had never seen his father in
a business suit except perhaps on Sunday when he goes to
church and puts on his Sunday clothes. Such a child would
give the correct answer from his own experience but he
would flunk that question and he would do badly on other
questions in the test with similar, though less obvious biases.
The child who would do well on these tests would be the ones
whose parents were engaged in conventional, traditional, acceptable middle class occupations. For example, my children would get the right answer. "Yes, the man in the business suit. That's the man going to work. That's the way
daddy goes to work." They have become, in that sense,
white middle class.

        The failure of our educational system creates brutal
statistics that vary little from ghetto to ghetto. For example, 87 percent of the children who actually graduate from
high school in the Bedford-Stuyvesant area of New York City
receive a general diploma, not an academic diploma which
would prepare one for college, or a technical diploma which
prepares one for vocational school, or a commercial diploma
which would prepare one to work in an office. A general
diploma prepares them for nothing but a dead end. But that
poor student comes out waving that piece of paper saying,
"I'm going to make it now. Just watch me. I wasn't a fool
like ole Andy who dropped out. I stayed in and served my
time." So he goes downtown to get a job and finds out that
he can't even fill out the job application blank. He has been
cheated, robbed, and humiliated.

        I think our educational systems have been oriented to
work against the poor, the black and the brown. I think this
must be changed and I think that the place to start is in
teacher training. Few teachers have been trained to teach
in ghettos. By and large the teacher training practices in
our country continue to prepare teachers to teach white,
middle-class, urban youngsters. There is nothing wrong
with being white, middle-class or urban, but there are many
children who are none of these things, and if the teacher is
not prepared to teach them then they are bound to fail in
school and in life. If a person does not have confidence in
the capacity of the pupils to learn, that person cannot teach.
Children cannot learn in such a class. Skin color has little
to do with such attitudes. I heard a black teacher speaking
to other black teachers in Harlem ask: "Why do you sweat?
Don't you know you're not training kids to go to Harvard?"
I say that teacher could not teach because his attitude would

communicate itself to his children very quickly. If there is
one thing that poor children quickly develop, it is sensitive
antennae. This teacher, by his attitude, is confirming what
society had said to the youngster all of his life and to his
parents all of their lives--that he is worthless and is going
no place. This teacher is saying what Jensen has said to
him. Is it any wonder that children in his class would
quickly pull down the curtain of learning.

        The teacher must be familiar with the life-style and
living conditions from which his children come. I do not believe that a teacher, in order to teach black children, has to
be black; or to teach Chicano kids has to be Chicano, and ad
infinitum. But I do believe it is essential that there be a
rapport between teacher and pupil. And that rapport cannot
exist unless the teacher is familiar with the life-style, the
living conditions and the community problems from which the
children come. The black teacher may have an advantage at
the outset because the black child may say, "there's a sister,
there's a brother. We are going to learn something. " But
if the teacher does not communicate and looks down his nose
at his students, he quickly dissipates that advantage because
there is nothing worse than one who is considered to be a
traitor. So the black teacher who dissipates that advantage
becomes the traitor. The white teacher standing before a
class of blacks, Chicanos or Puerto Ricans has many factors
working against him. They are suspicious of him. He is on
trial. If there is a test given, it is the teacher who is being tested. The teacher who is sufficiently sensitive and who
understands the lives of his students can overcome the difficulties and become an effective teacher.

        Another area of conflict in education centers on the
relationship of teacher unions and community groups. There
appears to be a collision course between legitimate demands
of the community and traditional demands of teacher unions.
For example, the community is saying, "we want teachers to
know that there is community. Teachers can visit the homes
from which their kids come and talk with the parents. "
Teachers say: "When? What time is there? It's three
o'clock, the day is over. " I say it can be done after school.

        The community says: "Listen, we want the best,
most experienced teachers assigned to our schools. " That is
a legitimate demand because poor children face many obstacles to learning. If they are going to learn they must
have the best teachers. The old trade unionist says: "Ex-

perienced teachers should go to where he wants to teach. "
Of course, the senior teachers choose the easiest places to
teach and those schools are not in the inner city.

The community says: "We want community control of
the schools. If a teacher does not perform, we want to fire
him. " But the trade unionist says: "No! There must be
job security. " We must sit down and have dialogue between
teacher groups and community groups. We must find ways
to enable teachers to become familiar with the life conditions
of the community. For example, if little Johnny seems in-
solent in class, it may be that he is hungry because he did
not have breakfast, because there was nothing in the refrig-
erator. The teacher must be sensitive to this fact. If Adam
falls asleep, it may not be that Adam has a short concentration span. Perhaps, Adam did not get any sleep the previous
night because the five, six or eight children living in that
two-room tenement flat were screaming, crying and fighting.
If Sammy does not do his homework, it may not be that he
lacks motivation. Perhaps there is no place for him to do
it. Perhaps, there was no table with a light on it. There
may not be any heat in the winter. If a teacher is to teach
and teach well, he or she must be familiar with these possibilities.

I think it is absolutely essential that we begin to tackle
these problems now. Earlier I said that I do not envy educators. For even if the notion of accountability is not accepted nationally, the communities and the parents of the
children we teach are going to hold educators accountable for
their product. I believe in accountability, which is why I am
in favor of the voucher system. I would be opposed to using
the voucher system throughout the country. But I think we
have got to experiment with it. The voucher system would
result in federal funds being given not to the school systems
or to the state departments of education--but directly to the
parents in the form of vouchers. The parents then are able
to send their children to whatever school they want them to
attend, either private or public, while paying for it with a
voucher. This system, hopefully, would not support those
private academies that the South has used in the effort to
evade desegregation. A school should be required to be integrated. It should have to select at least half of its pupils
through a lottery system from among those who applied, and
it would have no smaller percentage of minority groups in its
student body than have applied for admission. Other safe-
guards can also be built in. But I think that competition

among schools will make our educational system more accountable.

I would like to make a final point concerning the great
responsibility of schools in coming to understand the new
mood in the minority community. This new mood is one that
is demanding identity, pride and dignity. We used to tell
blacks, "Forget that you are a member of a group. Just
think of yourself as an individual. And if as an individual
you can get a little money and a little education then you will
be assimilated. Then you will become a white man, with
invisible black skin." That was the ideal held out to blacks
and other minorities in the past. But it did not work. The
United States is not a color blind nation. We tried to be
color blind but we failed. We would say to an employer,
"Be color blind." It did not work because when we went
back to him two years later and asked: "How many blacks
and Puerto Ricans do you employ?" He would say, "How
should I know? I'm color blind." An official check would
show he had none. He would say, "See, I'm color blind."

No, the nation is not color blind. One does not become color blind by wishing it so or by saying it is so.
Today there is nothing wrong with a black saying, "Black is
beautiful. It's wonderful to be black." Contrast that with
the old syndrome of the black saying, "I ain't nothing." I
would suggest that Americans have been so conditioned in our
country that it is extremely difficult for any of them, white
or black, to grow to adulthood without residues of that
racist conditioning existing within him. Now, when I hear
children say "black is beautiful" I say "right on!" It is so
much better not only to come to terms with self and accept
self but to sing the praises of self. To honor, to celebrate
me. I am great. I am somebody, because I am. It is an
honor to be born whatever one is born, so long as it is not
considered a dishonor to be born something else. What is
the difference between saying it is an honor to be born an
Irishman and saying black is beautiful? It is wonderful to
be black, just as it is wonderful to be Irish. I think that
the institutions of education have greater responsibility than
any other institution in helping to place that newfound pride
and identity in the context of a pluralistic culture. It is
great to be me. That does not mean that it is shameful and
wrong to be somebody else. Black is beautiful. What color
isn't? But it is important for me, when I have been kicked
and stood upon, to be able to say "I am beautiful and it is
good to be me." That does not mean that what is not black

is ugly.   It merely means that black is not ugly, as we have
been told for so many years.   But what is a pluralistic society?   We used to think the schools had a responsibility to
make people forget about groups.   That was the color blind
myth.   Our nation is not a melting pot.   It is a pluralistic
society.   I think the sooner we rid ourselves of the notion
that we are a melting pot, the sooner we will be able to
cope effectively with these problems.   We are a pluralistic
society.   When I was invited to be an honorary member of
the Italian-American Veterans club on the lower east side of
New York, I accepted with pleasure.   I consider that pluralistic culture.   Every St. Patrick's day I become a little bit
Irish.   Blacks will have really arrived when they can make
whites honorary Afro-Americans on some future Martin
Luther King Day.   America needs a pluralistic society, a
society which must be prepared now by educators.   Rabbi
Hillel expressed the urgency of this so beautifully when he
said: "If I am not for myself, who will be for me?   If I
am for myself alone, what am I?   And if not now, when?"

9. PREJUDICE AND THE GHETTO CHILD

by Sheldon Marcus

Belief in the allrightness of blackness prepares
a young black to go on and be somebody.   It gets
him ready to move about among other people,
whatever their color or special group, getting an
education, having a job, living in a neighborhood
and having his say about it and his country.   It
is not meant to hem him in with blacks, but to
stand him up and start him off to wherever he
would go.   So having his black sisters and brothers
may not alone be enough for him.   He may want
to take from his country and his world, the best
they have to offer and to give them back what he
can learn to provide like no one else can.   He
may want to do so, in part, to add to the pride
and comfort of black people and to help his country
to keep its biggest promise before the world.   He
may simply want to keep on trying out "whitey, "
as long as "whitey" keeps on saying, "to every
man the right to live, to work, to be himself,
and to become whatever thing his manhood and
his vision can combine to make him. "

George B. Nesbitt
The Crisis, December 1970

Unfortunately, many children confront prejudice of all
kinds within the school, an institution supposedly dedicated to
the elimination of bigotry.   It has been pointed out that equal
opportunity in education is a "legal myth. "   In essence, our
public schools, although open to all to attend, are biased in
favor of the middle and upper classes.

In "Elmtown, " a small mid-western city, the board
of education "did not conceive of the education of the lower
classes as part of their responsibility. "   More significantly,
the lower classes were not deemed important enough to be

89

represented on the board. The child of the lower class had
to be satisfied with a lower grade simply because he was a
member of a minority group. Again, lack of high social
status was equated with lack of achievement. In "Jonesville, " a cornbelt city, social class also determined the
grading system. "Teachers in Jonesville soon learned 'who
is who' and what must be done to satisfy the people who
count in the community. "[1]

But prejudice has had its most profound effect on the
inner city children of America's large cities, particularly
black children. In the minutes of a meeting parents and
students of a school in a Chicago ghetto the following complaints were voiced:

> The teachers treated the white and wealthy black
> students differently than they treated the rest of
> the black students.... Mr. C stepped on a boy's
> toes, the boy spoke up, was sent to the office and
> suspended.... He let 'Toms' get away with mur-
> der.... Mrs. A insults the kids. Calls the
> parents uneducated, belittles those on welfare, pre-
> dicts that the girls will be having babies and boys
> on the corner using dope and drinking wine. Mr.
> B pushes on the children and knocks them around
> .... Mr. D hit a boy and invited him to the gym
> to fight.... If a white kid is around with black
> kids, the teachers pick on them.... The teacher
> does not explain the work ... doesn't answer
> questions.[2]

Additional insight into the nature of racial prejudice
was noted by Kenneth B. Clark in his work Prejudice And
Your Child. He stated that "The more prejudiced the individual the less he will be able to modify his behavior when
objective conditions require it; that prejudiced individuals
have a more constricted range of general interests.... "[3]
Clark also stated that these people have a limited amount of
personal insight, and are generally less original in their
thinking.[4] An example of this may be seen by looking at
one of Jonathan Kozol's experiences in his Death at an Early
Age. He describes his confrontation with a reading teacher
in the school in the following manner:

> I remember a day when she had come up into my
> classroom during lunchtime. She was in one of
> her moods of exposing the bigotry of other teachers

> while at the same time rather pridefully extolling
> her own virtues. 'Others may be prejudiced, ' she
> was saying to me. 'So and so downstairs uses
> the word "nigger. " I know, I've heard him say
> it with my own ears. It makes me sick every
> time I hear him say that. If a person feels that
> way I don't know what he's doing teaching at this
> school....'5

This particular reading teacher claimed that when she looked
at her students she did not see white or black, but only a
boy or a girl. "White skin or black skin, they all are made
by God. " The same reading teacher, however, once refused
to dance with a black man. "I knew it was wrong but I
honestly could not make myself say yes to that man. It was
because he was a Negro. I just could not see myself danc-
ing with that man. "6

The advancement of blacks has been particularly
hampered by segregation and discrimination which have either
denied them access to formal education or relegated them to
inadequate schools. Kozol noted some very shocking items
about the school system in Boston. In regard to school
budget, in schools with all-white student enrollments, approximately $350 per pupil per year was allocated. Per pupil
expenditure in heavily populated Negro districts, however,
was approximately $240. Also, 10 percent lower textbook
expenditures were allocated in the black schools of Boston.
Similar figures were shown in the area of health and library
expenditures. 7 Yet, many people living in this area felt that
the Boston school system was doing very well. "The schools
are doing a wonderful job with what they've got. You take
these kids from homes like those and parents from all over
... how on earth do you expect a day in school to change
that child's life?"8 It seemed as though it were the inferior
students rather than the inferior teachers who were responsible for the educational problems in the community. "But
these men are your brothers--your lost, younger brothers.
And if the word integration means anything, this is what it
means: that we, with love, shall force our brothers to see
themselves as they are, to cease fleeing from reality and
begin to change it. "9

James Herndon also described the attitude of some of
the bigoted teachers in his school in his The Way It Spozed
to Be.

> Skates was a big young guy, twenty-six or so,
> from Chicago, and if there was anything he really
> hated it was teaching school. ... Skates called
> our students THE TRIBE. Watch out today, he'd
> yell to me coming down the hall for lunch. The
> Tribe's getting edgy! Or, come into my room,
> the Tribe's holding a talent show, tap-dancing,
> strippers, the whole bit! It's a little gift from
> me, in appreciation they didn't eat me up last
> week![10]

This humorous work brought forth some of the menial
assignments which teachers required their students to perform, simply because they felt the students were not capable
of intellectual stimulation. Some teachers merely instructed
their students to copy from the blackboard paragraphs which
they had constructed. This was the extent of the lessons.
"School tends to be a dishonest as well as a nervous place.
We adults are not often honest with children, least of all in
school. We tell them, not what we think, but what we feel
they ought to think; or what other people feel or tell us they
ought to think."[11]

Kenneth B. Clark in Dark Ghetto speaks of certain
false assumptions which some educators make. For example,

> it is not really worth it to put time and effort
> into teaching blacks because, after all 'they' will
> only become frustrated. There is no point in
> 'their' having high academic aspirations since
> 'their lives will be restricted to menial jobs. ...
> The humanitarian thing to do for these children,
> the proponents of such theories maintain, is to
> provide schools that are essentially custodial,
> rather than educational institutions. [12]

However, as Herbert Kohl pointed out in 36 Children, minority children are capable of learning if the teacher is
willing to give of himself to his class. Kohl took his students on trips on which he let them use their own imagina-
tions and as a result, the students constructed their own
books. They also created a school paper entitled AND.
But, as one teacher once told Kohl, "One good year isn't
enough. ... "[13]

Racial prejudice has for a long time caused the black

man to humble himself. The familiar "Uncle Tom" image
emerged as a means to cope with the "psychic drainage system" of slavery. The black man has experienced a type of
identity crisis. The concept of self-image has come to the
foreground. This identity crisis was portrayed by Ralph
Ellison in his novel The Invisible Man.

> No, I am not a spook like those who haunted Edgar
> Allan Poe; nor am I one of Hollywood movie ecto-
> plasms. I am a man of substance, of flesh and
> bone, fiber and liquids--and I might even be said
> to possess a mind. I am invisible, understand,
> simply because people refuse to see me....
>
> Nor is my invisibility exactly a matter of bio-
> chemical accidents to my epidermis. That invis-
> ibility to which I refer occurs because of a pecul-
> iar disposition of the eyes of those with whom I
> come in contact.... You wonder whether you
> aren't simply a phantom in other people's minds
> .... And, let me confess, you feel that way most
> of the time. You ache with the need to convince
> yourself that you do exist in the real world ...
> you curse and you swear to make them recognize
> you. And, also, it's seldom successful. [14]

This search for identity is related to the discussion involving
a proper group name for these people.

> The debate has been bound up with the ways in
> which black Americans have tried to find a place
> in the white society which has so consistently and
> completely excluded them.... [T]he confusion and
> controversy over name is bound up with the most
> fundamental question of identity: the flight from
> blackness, the hatred of self, the yearning to be
> white. [15]

Traditionally, white has been the symbol of good, and black
has been linked to that which is evil. This image has had
its effect upon the black man's self-image. He views himself as being locked in chains by a white society. This sense
of worthlessness and hostility is witnessed in Richard
Wright's Native Son. Bigger Thomas and Gus are peering
at a plane in the sky.

> 'You can hardly see it, ' Gus said. 'Looks like a

little bird, ' Bigger breathed with childlike wonder.
'Them white boys sure can fly, ' Gus said. 'Yeah, '
Bigger said wistfully.   They get a chance to do
everything. ...   Maybe they right in not wanting us
to fly ... 'cause if I took a plane up I'd take a
couple of bombs along and drop 'em sure as hell
.... '16

This hostility is further perpetuated by some men and
women in the education system who continue to refer to their
students as "animals in a zoo. " Such hostility has prompted
Dick Gregory in his work Nigger to state that:

You didn't die a slave for nothing, Momma.   You
brought us up. ...   Those of us who weren't destroyed got stronger, got calluses on our souls.
And now we're ready to change a system, a system where a white man can destroy a black man
with a single word.   Nigger. 17

Regardless of the reasons we give, the blacks are
revolting against a society dominated by whites, a society in
which they find it very difficult to succeed.   One can almost
feel the anger bursting forth from Eldridge Cleaver: "We
shall have our manhood.   We shall have it or the earth will
be leveled by our attempts to gain it. "18

Children of Hispanic American background also are
confronted with many distinct obstacles.   For example, some
Puerto Ricans are discriminated against because of their
color.   The dark-skinned Puerto Rican in his native sur-
roundings does not envision the concept of "civil rights" as
the contemporary black American does.   The need for such
a movement is not prevalent in Puerto Rico.   Thus, in the
United States, the Puerto Rican is often misunderstood by
blacks in situations relating to racial matters.

This dilemma has also been pointed out by Oscar
Handlin in his work The Newcomers.

If color consciousness grows more intense and the
penalties of identification of color grow more
severe, the Puerto Rican group may be fragmented
into three parts.   The continuing flow of new arri-
vals will struggle to maintain themselves as Puerto
Ricans.   The colored Puerto Ricans already settled, and particularly those of the second and third

generations for whom the difference of language
fades in importance, will be pressed toward an
identification with the more numerous Negroes.
And the white majority of second and third generation Puerto Ricans who lose the consciousness
of language will find an ever-growing incentive to
drop their identification and to merge with some
other surrounding ethnic community. [19]

The problem of racial prejudice provided the impetus
towards these words by Piri Thomas:

I got a feeling of aloneness and bittorncoo
    that's growing and growing
Day by day into some kind of hate without
    "un nombre" [a name]
Yet when I look down at the streets below,
    I can't help thinking
It's like a great big dirty Christmas tree
    with lights but no ... presents ...
What have you got now? Nothing.
What will you ever have? Nothing ... [20]

One means of attacking the problems of the newcomers is through the educational system.   But, certain
false assumptions and prejudices which some educators hold
must be overcome.   Since most of the newcomers flock to
the city, the urban schools will be confronted with the necessity of meeting the needs of these minority groups.

Today, there is a movement of the middle class from
the city to the suburbs, a trend which will continue for some
time. With the flight of the middle class, the cities will embrace the very rich and the very poor.   The rich parents
will make use of the private schools to provide their children with an eduation.   The poor will continue to send their
offspring to public schools which will shortly service only the
children of the poor.

There are a number of ways in which the urban
schools can face the challenge of educating these groups.
One such way is to diversify the ethnic and racial make-up
of the teaching staff of urban schools.   Teachers who speak
and understand the language of the children they are teaching
would alleviate some of the language difficulties which face
the pupil.   Warner Saunders, a black who runs Chicago's
Better Boys Foundation, is trying to improve the schools by

educating the teachers to get rid of racist principals and by
helping to write a more meaningful curriculum for ghetto
schools.   He is concerned about teacher animosity to non-
standard English.   "If I tamper with a person's first language, I'm suggesting that all he has been and felt in the
past is bad. "[21]

        The textbooks used in the urban schools should also
meet the needs of the pupils instead of mirroring the culture
of WASP America.   The experience background of the student could be expanded through the use of slides, tapes,
teaching machines, and other audio-visual devices.   Well-
trained guidance counselors could be of great assistance in
directing the pupils to proper occupational choices.   More
fundamentally, in order to improve the quality of urban education one must first improve the quality of the teacher in
the urban school.   Learning about teaching in the urban
ghetto is no substitute for actual classroom experience.

        The urban teacher must realize that the blacks through
the years of deprivation have developed their own "ghetto
ethic" which serves as a "composite credo for the ghetto
life styles. "[22]   He cannot and should not destroy that ethic
by his conscious or unconscious prejudices.   Ghetto schools
are different and should be accepted as such; middle class
education in the ghetto is deemed irrelevant.   The drama
of middle-class America is not a reality for the children of
the ghetto.   Neither is its language.   And learning for the
sake of learning holds no motivation for the ghetto child.
The school, at best,

                provides comedy relief from intolerable home and
                life situations.   The students learn early how best
                to turn the school scene to what they think is their
                advantage.   Most are capable of creating only bed-
                lam; all things emotional prevail.   The atmosphere
                is so mentally scattering and exhausting that any
                problem or subject that requires concentration is
                too difficult.   Thinking is, after all, hard work.
                Their substitute for application to academic goals
                is a witty frivolity, for there is humor in the
                ghetto as well as sordidness. [23]

        A child in the ghetto must learn to live in and cope
with his environment.   In order to do this he must often be
rough and tough.   He has no use for the quiet, gentle man-
ners of the middle class.   If he held to these ways he would

not survive long in his neighborhood. When he gets to school
where middle-class values and patterns of behavior are
favored, he is continually chastised. The alert teacher
should pick out the skills that the child has learned living in
the ghetto environment and apply them to his teaching, thereby making the material more relevant and easing behavior
problems at the same time.

The ghetto child starts school on the wrong foot. He
attends schools staffed by inferior teachers, many of whom
may not be able to help him or may be unwilling to help
him. "Small deficiencies at an early age lead to inferior
learning which in turn increases the magnitude of the deficiency."[24] The ghetto child does not lack the ability to
learn. He has not been given the chance to develop his
proper potential. It is rare, if ever, that the teacher will
sit down with the under-achiever and find out what makes
him tick. Most ghetto children bear great burdens at home.
They come to school and cannot relate to the subjects being
taught. No child who is hungry or sleepy can learn. Often,
even if the child is interested in learning, family conditions
make it nearly impossible for him to get any work done at
home, so he comes into school unprepared, unable to succeed, and frustrated. His self-image is a deterent to his
learning.

The school offers little help. The ghetto schools are
shortchanged in all aspects. They receive less money per
child than do middle-class schools. The physical facilities
are often run down. Teacher turnover is phenomenal. Usually, it is the least experienced teacher who must cope with
the most difficult teaching problems. Many teachers feel
that the ghetto child cannot learn and this is reflected in
their dealings with the children. The children are held back,
placed in low-level, slow-progress classes, and channeled
into non-academic terminal secondary school programs.
These courses of action, in many cases, lead to the reaffir-
mation and aggravation of low achievement.

William Perel and Philip Vairo have said:

> The teacher, the central figure in the learning
> process, has not been willing to learn and appre-
> ciate the problems associated with the slum culture
> of the lower class pupil. The teacher has lacked
> any real understanding of the lower class pupil's
> world. The emphasis in our present educational

> system is to make the lower class student conform
> to middle class values. The teacher, a mature
> "educated" individual, assumes the task of bring-
> ing the lower class youngster up to standard.
> There is no attempt on the part of the school to
> utilize the experiences the lower class youngster
> brings from his slum culture. Is it taboo? ...
> The school fails to utilize the experiences of the
> lower class youngsters thereby denying them the
> opportunity to participate in school activities.
> Lower class children come to a middle class in-
> stitution, surrounded by middle class minded
> teachers, and must conform to a behavior pattern
> and goals that are foreign to them. In essence,
> the lower class youth is penalized from the very
> first day he enters school if he does not conform
> to the middle class way of life. The current
> crisis in American education is due not only to
> the lower class child's alienation from the school,
> but perhaps equally to the teacher's inadequate
> training to work with culturally deprived students.
> There is a need for prospective teachers to have
> a crusading zeal for helping the socially under-
> privileged child. [25]

One result of discrimination is that even those people
who do acquire middle-class status have been prevented from
moving out of the ghetto to enjoy the fruits of their effort.
This fact effectively destroys the influence of parents attempting to inculcate in their children the belief that they
can succeed in the world if they work hard and get a good
education.

How will we improve the quality of urban education
and overcome the impact of prejudice? How can the children who are the victims of poverty and discrimination grow
to maturity with mind and soul whole and undestroyed? Will
giving the poor the means to control their own education
help achieve this? Is black power the key answer? We believe that the elimination of the forces of stratification and
segregation is the goal that must be achieved to make the
inner city different from what it has become. Therefore,
the students in the inner city must be placed in classes that
are as little class-stratified as possible. We need compensatory education. We need smaller classes, relevant curricula and instructional methods, better-trained teachers and
administrators, relevant teacher-training programs, and

greater use of para-professionals. Most of all, because we
cannot solve the problems of the world instantly, we must
make all teachers aware of the sensitivities and cultural
heritage of minority groups. Through understanding, prejudice can be eroded and children's minds can be made to
grow in a healthy manner until that time when they teach us
how all men may live as equals.

References

1. William M. Perel and Philip D. Vairo, Urban Education: Problems and Prospects, New York: David
McKay, 1969; p. 59.

2. Newsweek. June 9, 1969; p. 42.

3. Kenneth B. Clark, Prejudice and Your Child, Boston:
Beacon Press, 1963; p. 70.

4. Ibid.

5. Jonathan Kozol, Death at an Early Age, Boston:
Houghton-Mifflin, 1967; p. 21.

6. Ibid., p. 21-23.

7. Ibid., p. 54.

8. Ibid.

9. James Baldwin, The Fire Next Time, New York: Dial,
1963; p. 21.

10. James Herndon, The Way It Spozed to Be, New York:
Bantam Books, 1968; p. 51-55.

11. John Holt, How Children Fail, New York: Pitman, 1964;
p. 170.

12. Kenneth Clark, Dark Ghetto, New York: Harper and
Row, 1965; p. 126-127.

13. Herbert Kohl, 36 Children, New York: New American
Library, 1967; p. 3-180.

14. Ralph Ellison, The Invisible Man, New York: Signet
     Books, 1947; p. 7-8.

15. Charles E. Silberman, Crisis in Black and White,
     New York: Random House, 1964; p. 112-114.

16. Richard Wright, Native Son, New York: Harper and
     Row, 1957; p. 19-20.

17. Dick Gregory, Nigger, New York: Dutton, 1965; p. 209.

18. Eldridge Cleaver, Soul on Ice, New York: Dell, 1968;
     p. 9.

19. Oscar Handlin, The Newcomers, Cambridge, Mass.:
     Harvard University Press, 1959; p. 61.

20. Piri Thomas, Down These Mean Streets,   New York:
     Signet Books, 1967; prologue.

21. Newsweek, op. cit., p. 42.

22. Brian Neal Odell, "The Ghetto Ethic," The Catholic
     World, February 1970; p. 214.

23. B. E. Patrick, "Ghetto Schools Are Different,"
     National Review, April 21, 1970; p. 402.

24. Carl Bereiter and Seigfried Engelmann, Teaching Dis-
     advantaged Children in the Preschool, Englewood
     Cliffs, N. J.: Prentice-Hall, 1966; p. 5.

25. Perel and Vairo, op. cit., p. 12.

10. MEETING THE NEEDS OF AMERICA'S DISADVANTAGED

by Herman Badillo

In the 1960's there were many of us who thought that the major educational problem in America was that our nation did not know what to do about the disadvantaged. Therefore, we accepted speaking engagements and wrote numerous proposals in which we explained what needed to be done about the disadvantaged. Thus, if one looks at the record of the 1960's one will find volumes telling exactly what to do to solve the problems of our underprivileged population. We thought we knew exactly what to do about housing--new houses had to be constructed and old houses rehabilitated. Yet housing continues to deteriorate. Several years ago I suggested that since landlords no longer wanted to be in the real estate business in the slum areas and the city did not have the resources to manage the buildings, tenants should be allowed to take over the buildings. It is interesting to note that this proposal was praised even by the New York Daily News. But, of course, nothing more happened.

We have become accustomed to the idea that proposals submitted to various government agencies to alleviate the suffering of the poor are praised and welcomed and then are usually promptly forgotten. This phenomenon occurs in every area of urban life where solutions have been proposed. For example, in education we have prepared a number of proposals which show that black and Puerto Rican children can achieve a high level of attainment, can graduate with an academic diploma from high school and go on to college. But the proposals are not implemented. We have talked about bilingual education for a long period of time and I was one of those who supported it. The first bilingual school in the City of New York was established in the Bronx when I was borough president. But a year after the bilingual school was established, it still had not received any financial support from the federal government. Today there are only two bilingual schools in New York City. We are really just playing games. It is regrettable that although the bilingual school has been successful no concerted effort has been made

to establish bilingual schools in New York City or elsewhere.
It is not a question of not knowing how to solve educational
problems.   Rather, it is a question of not wanting to make
the commitment to do so.   There is no commitment on the
part of government to take action to solve the problems of
education.   It is not lack of insight but a lack of will and a
lack of a desire to make the necessary investment to solve
the problems of our day.   We will continue to make proposals from time to time to solve the problems which face our
cities, but I do not seriously believe that there is going to
be a massive movement to take the necessary action.

I want to give one example of how the United States
as a country has failed to meet the needs of the disadvantaged, and I am going to use the Puerto Rican community in
Puerto Rico and in New York as the example.   As for myself, I was born in Puerto Rico and lived there until I was
11 years of age, after which I became part of Puerto Rican
society in New York City.   I believe I speak from personal
experience.   It should also be remembered that the Puerto
Ricans have many of the characteristics of all the disadvantaged.   There are white Puerto Ricans; there are black
Puerto Ricans; there are racially mixed Puerto Ricans.
Puerto Ricans as Latins have many of the characteristics of
Mexican Americans.   But the Puerto Ricans as distinguished
from the Mexican Americans have come predominantly to the
large urban centers, not to the Southwest or to the rural
areas of America.   Thus, the Puerto Rican group is a prime
example of what our urban minority poor face in the urban
centers.

Because Puerto Rico became a part of the U. S. in
1898, we have a history of many decades on which to review
the kind of action the United States has taken in its dealings
with a distinctly disadvantaged population.   We can divide the
relationships between Puerto Rico and the rest of American
society into two historical periods.   The first period dates
from 1898 to 1932, and that was really a period of almost
total colonialism where Puerto Rico was governed by governors appointed by the President of the United States without
consultation with the Puerto Rican community.   During this
period there were no proposals whatsoever to help the Puerto
Rican community other than the Jones Act of 1917, which
granted Puerto Ricans American citizenship.   The reason
for this was that the entry of the United States into World
War I created a need for men to be drafted into the armed
forces.   The only way Puerto Ricans could be drafted into

the United States armed forces was to make them citizens.
Other than this action, there were no programs designed to
help the Puerto Ricans achieve the level of income of the
average American.   During this entire period Puerto Rico
was owned and monopolized by huge corporations who ran the
country as a plantation.   There was no real effort to develop
an effective educational program for the people of Puerto
Rico.

The second period covered the years from 1932 to
1944, which was the era of the New Deal.   The Roosevelt
Administration attempted to recognize that the United States
had a responsibility to Puerto Rico.   Thus, there were programs like the Work Projects Administration that were developed for the United States, but which were, for the first
time, also implemented in Puerto Rico.   Such programs
helped to bring about at least a minimum standard of health
care in Puerto Rico and prevented economic disaster on the
Island.   Of course, there still were not enough jobs in
Puerto Rico and to help solve the unemployment problem it was
decided to give Puerto Rico a measure of self-government.
It was only during the latter part of this period that Puerto
Rico was able to reach an agreement with the United States
under which the people of Puerto Rico could elect their own
legislature.   When Puerto Ricans began to develop a program of economic development, it was a program quite
limited in scope.   Because the economy of Puerto Rico had
been neglected for such a long time, the number of jobs that
were created by the popularly elected Puerto Rican government was far smaller than the number of people who were
in the labor force.   The only reason that Puerto Rico was
able to survive in the period from 1944 to 1960 was simply
because of the mass migration to the United States.

The Puerto Rican exodus is not a migration of people
who are escaping political or religious persecution.   It is a
migration of people seeking economic opportunity, not people
seeking welfare.   The Puerto Ricans who came here were
young.   Even today, the medium age of the Puerto Rican
coming to the states is less than 21 years.   The migration
of the young always is a migration of people who cannot find
opportunity where they are and consequently they seek opportunity elsewhere.

In the past 30 years approximately one million people
have left Puerto Rico for the mainland.   This is indeed a
huge migration.   It is the equivalent of 40 million Americans

leaving the United States.   Thus, we must not be too enthu-
siastic when we say that the government of Puerto Rico has
had tremendous success with its Operation Boot Strap.   Although the Puerto Rican government was able to attract new
industries and create jobs, the major reason the standard of
living of the Puerto Rican improved was because of the mass
migration to the mainland.   Puerto Ricans who came to the
mainland seeking opportunities soon found themselves caught
in the urban crisis.   They were aware that there were no
programs to help Puerto Ricans in Puerto Rico.   They soon
discovered that there were no programs on the mainland to
help overcome the poverty in our cities.   The government of
the United States simply has not recognized the urban problem as a national problem.

        The Puerto Ricans who now come to the mainland
find that factory jobs are being eliminated.   Additionally,
hundreds of thousands of jobs are being lost by the cities to
the suburbs.   Blacks and Puerto Ricans are moving into the
cities at the very time that industry is leaving many urban
centers, especially in the East.   This is a serious disadvantage confronting Puerto Ricans and Blacks which the Irish,
Italians and the Jews and other ethnic groups who migrated
to the United States many years ago were not confronted
with.   Years ago man could find employment if all he had to
offer was muscle, because most of the work of our society
was then done by muscle.   Today most of the work of our
society is done by machines, and therefore we really have
no use for people who are not specially trained.   Puerto
Ricans also have a language problem that poses an additional
disadvantage that even the blacks that come from the South
do not face.   Puerto Ricans also face the problems posed by
an educational system that has not rendered satisfactory
service to the Puerto Rican community.   For example, when
I attended Haaren High School I learned how to take an airplane engine apart.   That was a World War II vintage and
those engines are still in Haaren High School.   Yet, nobody
would think of flying such a plane but nevertheless children
are still learning to take these airplane engines apart as if
this could be a meaningful and a legitimate professional experience.

        Many Puerto Ricans are steered into vocational or
general programs only to find that when they complete the
course of study they are several years behind in reading and that they really do not possess any marketable skills.
In my case I happened to learn to speak English in time to

go on to the City College of New York, but I did not receive
any counseling from the school system.   Unfortunately, very
little guidance is available today.   I have visited schools at
which principals and teachers have encouraged parents to
send their children to attend vocational schools by telling
them that it is not possible for their children to obtain an
academic diploma and to attend a college or university.

This same pattern applies in the area of housing.
The Puerto Rican community has tried to develop programs
in housing but nobody is building housing any longer in our
cities.   Puerto Ricans have large families and even where
there is housing built by the city, it is not designed for these
large families.   So Puerto Ricans find themselves living
in the worst housing conditions in the cities.

There is one other aspect I want to discuss about the
Puerto Rican experience--the mass migration of Puerto Ricans to the mainland.   Since 1960 there has been a continued migration, but it is evident from the figures released
by the Commonwealth of Puerto Rico that there is a reverse
migration of Puerto Ricans leaving New York City and other
cities and returning to Puerto Rico.   For example, in 1971,
there was a net influx of 25,000 people returning to Puerto
Rico from the mainland.   Such figures are detrimental to
the cities of America, because the Puerto Ricans who go
back to the Island are the individuals who have developed
skills: college graduates, doctors, lawyers, or architects.
Basically, the Puerto Rican who returns to Puerto Rico has
a middle-class orientation while the Puerto Rican who comes
to the mainland is poor and lacks marketable skills and education.   The Puerto Ricans that one sees in New York City,
Hartford, Chicago, and other parts of this country are usually the poor Puerto Ricans.   No other Puerto Rican who
has his senses would want to leave Puerto Rico.

Middle-class white America usually only has occasion
to meet uneducated migrants and that leads to a wrong impression of the Puerto Rican community.   Because people do
not meet Puerto Rican doctors, lawyers, architects, authors,
or philosophers in New York City, they assume that they
don't exist.   They do exist but they are in Puerto Rico.
Many Puerto Ricans in our cities sense a feeling of inse-
curity and frustration because they only see that aspect of
the Puerto Rican social structure which is poor.   They do
not live in a society where the judges and the teachers are
all Puerto Rican or at least there is some ethnic represen-

tation.   Thus, they become impressed if a Puerto Rican becomes a principal in New York City or if a Puerto Rican
gets accepted into the plumbers or carpenters union.   But all
the plumbers in Puerto Rico are Puerto Rican and so are the
architects, the builders, and the contractors.

It should be remembered that Puerto Rico has been a
part of the United States since 1898 and still has a per-capita
income less than half the per-capita income in the state of
Mississippi, which ranks lowest among the 50 states and is
generally recognized as a disaster area.

The Puerto Ricans who live in the cities on the mainland have the lowest per-capita income of any group in the
society, including the blacks.   The per-capita income of
Puerto Ricans in New York City is far lower than that of
blacks.   Puerto Ricans rank low in terms of educational attainment and very high in terms of unemployment rates.
They are the victims of the conditions of poverty in our cities.
If this is what the United States has to offer Puerto Ricans,
one can begin to appreciate why it is that the people of Latin
America have lost faith in such slogans as the "good neighbor
policy. "

For the next ten years, the number of jobs created
in Puerto Rico is going to be far less than the number of
people going to join the labor force there.   This means that
either conditions will get worse in Puerto Rico or there will
have to be additional migration to the cities on the mainland.
We now know that additional migration to our cities will only
result in additional grief because there are really no programs to deal even with those Puerto Ricans who are living
in poverty now and certainly there will be no program for
those who may come later.   Yet, there is no attempt to coordinate efforts to deal with the urban problems.   Thus, I
have come to the conclusion that it really is going to take
generations to resolve our urban difficulties.

Ten or 15 years ago there were many of us who believed that perhaps the United States would learn from the
experience of the other groups who came here before the
Puerto Ricans.   But this was not to be the case.   Instead,
Americans are asking why Puerto Ricans should receive
special treatment when they or their parents had to work
hard without government assistance.   Puerto Ricans, on the
other hand, are American citizens and the reason they are in
the states is because of the expansionist and colonial policies

of the United States.   Thus, it is my opinion that the United
States has a responsibility to try to help Puerto Ricans
achieve in one generation what took other minorities perhaps
two or three lifetimes.   But this is not going to happen.
Puerto Ricans are going to have to "make it" in the same
slow way as other immigrants have in the past.   Eventually,
Puerto Ricans will achieve, but it is a tragedy that our nation has not learned from past experiences.   I think that this
situation diminshes the image of this country not only among
other Latin countries but before the world at large.

11. URBAN CRISES: SHALL WE OVERCOME?

by James R. Tanner

There really is no need for me to attempt to discuss
here all of the various dimensions of the massive crises
confronting every urban center across this nation and perhaps
across the world.   As a long-time school man, who believes
in the continued viability of the urban schools, I want to
share with you some of the mail I receive as assistant superintendent for curriculum and instruction in the Cleveland
public schools in order to give some insights into the problems which we face.   A year or so ago the superintendent
made a statement expressing concern over the nutritional
needs of pupils.   Of course, he received several letters in
the mail.   Although this letter was written on August 2, 1968,
I am sure that the lady would say it again today,

Dear Sir:

I'm writing in reference to a statement supposed to
have been made by you regarding the feeding of the starving children in Cleveland.   If this is the case, your city
should hang its head in shame.
Let me ask you where all these poor and starving children have come from all of a sudden.   My husband has been actively engaged in the real estate business for more than 40 years and with all his dealings
with hundreds of poor colored and white people he has
never found any at any time to be starving.   Perhaps not
enjoying expensive food, but not starving.   In my opinion
this condition is being exaggerated to the detriment of
us middle-class citizens and we're getting fed up to the
neck hearing about it in every broadcast.
Would you like to have a suggestion to pass on to
your colored mayor who promised so much to the poor?
Stop the flow of the poor and starving from the South to
Cleveland--I understand that they are coming in droves
into every city where they will eventually be on relief
and continue to have babies every wash day, which they
are unable to support.   They do not seem to require any

assistance in this procedure.

Again, in my humble opinion, you officials are
overlooking the basic causes in connection with all the
poverty programs.   You should hold meetings and
classes for these ignorant poor parents so an effort
might be made to stop the population explosion and ille-
gitimate soaring birth rate.   My husband has proof ga-
lore of this, not rightly sure how, but he does.   The
children are not to blame--in other words--these poor
people need much more than money, and I agree with
that.

What were all you school officials, the mayor and
councilmen, doing when you allowed the Hoff area to become the national disgrace that it did.   These lazy filthy
people should have been better citizens.

One last question.   What can you predict for the
poor when the money runs out?   And I'm sure it will in
the not too distant future.   As far as I'm concerned
black is still black, white is still white, and ambition
will never become obsolete.   According to LBJ, the
country has never been so prosperous; and still you have
starving children in Cleveland.

It was signed by a lady who came from a city not too far
from Cleveland, and I think it illustrates one of the real
hazards school personnel must deal with.

This next letter came from a lady to whom I think I
had been rude (and I'm not often rude to people).   She called
me on one of those difficult days when everybody has problems and I was not in the mood to listen to complaints, especially hers.   When I found out she was not a parent in our
school district I simply hung up.   Her letter follows:

Dear Mr. Tanner:

I was the lady you rudely hung up over the phone
Wednesday, June 24, 1970.   It seems that you were very
prejudiced against anybody who was white and who lives
in Cleveland Heights.

I originally called to have a conversation with you
but I soon found that you have no control of poise as far
as your disposition goes.   You are a very poor representative of public relations to the Cleveland Board of
Education.

I also own two businesses in Cleveland and pay taxes
which help pay your salary.   After talking to you, I have

decided to move my businesses to a suburb where my
tax money is needed.

I'm so glad to hear so many students go to college
now in Cleveland. I'm sure that many of their parents
don't need jobs from me. I must be mid-Victorian to
want employees who can follow orders, spell correctly,
speak clearly, and be able to do easy arithmetic. Anybody over 30 is considered a square nowadays. I know,
your voice sounds twice thirty, so maybe you should re-
tire. To let you in on a secret, business people who
have to earn double their money still want employees
that can add, subtract, and speak correctly in their
visits. It might be old fashioned, but the owners still
demand it. If you want your students to have jobs this
summer or when they graduate, you'd better rearrange
your curriculum for next fall.

I was educated during the depression. Teachers
were really good teachers then. Many had to work without pay. They had only the money parents could get together so they could eat and clothe themselves. Today,
you educators have it easy. Just take the taxpayers'
money and don't do any work.

Mr. Tanner, please watch your disposition. If
you get that temper up you are likely to have a stroke.
Why don't you take a course in the Cleveland schools on
public relations.

Please don't be such a bigot, everyone should live
together happily like we do in our community. Visit us
sometime and find how nice we can be. Thank you.

P. S. Good luck next fall and have a happy vacation.
Remember love your neighbor. I'm glad you had a
chance for a college degree, I didn't because I was a
depression youngster.

I suppose these missives might well be gathered in
any area of this nation where there is a big city and where
there are people who are resistant to cities, what cities
are and what they are going to become.

In another suburb of Cleveland called Euclid, where
75, 000 people live, the Board of Education several years
ago aired the demands submitted by the Euclid Citizen's
Council. These demands were:

... Spend tax money on Euclid students only.
... Permit parents to visit classes at any time.

... Submit book lists and curricula to the Citizens'
    Council for approval.
... Open to the public all school meetings.
... Investigate all subversive student organizations.
... Publish the names of all new teachers thirty days
    prior to employment.
... Prohibit the study of ethnic history without prior
    written consent of each individual parent.
... If Negro history is taught in our school, the his-
    tory of all national groups should be taught.
... Permit both sides of any issues to be discussed
    before the student and faculty groups.
... Tax money shall not be used for busing to obtain
    racial balance.

It seems to me that in the past several years there
has developed a great deal of confusion about the role of our
school. We either have unrealistic expectations for our
schools or our schools are not communicating to the public
and are not clarifying their role, scope, and mission.
People have come to expect the school to guarantee that
every child in the city is physically, mentally, and socially
well-adjusted, and adapted to his environment; that he has
proper respect for his elders and he is patriotic; that he is
knowledgeable about the social customs and that he's aware
of the dangers of drug abuse and the laws of the land; that
he is able to converse in both the native language and at
least one other; that he is able to perform in some vocational area; that he is prepared to enter a prestigious college; that he understands and defends the values of his
parents if not of the community at large, and that he will
come to appreciate the arts; and that the student be religious, kind, loyal, obedient, trustworthy, thrifty, well-
groomed, virtuous, properly nourished, and knowledgeable
about sex. The schools are also expected to help black
children learn how to be black. Recently I received a letter
from another nationality group in Cleveland which said the
schools also should teach all people ethnic studies. These
requests are fine, but we must recognize the fact that we
only have a certain amount of time in a day and, I may add,
limited funds.

There are many people who believe that the school
can build a new social order. The fact is that the school
cannot, never has been able to, and probably never will be
able by itself to build a new social order. Those who believe that the school can do so ignore the fact that the school

is only one of the agencies that is involved in the educational
process and it operates in partnership with other social institutions in the society, e. g., family, church, and government.   The school has been expected today to solve problems
it did not create and which it is not now or likely in the
future to be equipped to solve.

There are many suburbs which have developed since
the 1930's and have been a haven for whites who wanted to
escape the city.   These suburban schools are now expected
to solve the problems of segregation when the state and
federal governments for 30 years subsidized and indeed encouraged segregated housing.   I do not know of any school that
has the resources to rebuild the slums in its community.
No school is prepared to do that.   No school is prepared to
solve the problems associated with unemployment; no school
that I know of is prepared to solve the problems of urban
decay.   No school is equipped to solve the problems related
to inadequate health and medical care that is often found in
our cities.   The school cannot be all things to all people
and prepare students in the many areas of human knowledge.
I grow weary of the professors who themselves are probably
refugees from the responsibilities of the classroom and who
think they have all the answers to solve all the classroom
problems as well as those of society.   I also grow weary of
ineffectual teachers who wish to blame their failure on society and ignore their own inadequacies.   I grow equally
weary of social agencies which have decided to change their
role from that of serving people to that of organizing people
for or against one issue or another.   I do not know anybody
organizing people today for things, but I do know a good
many people who are organizing people against something and
especially against our schools because they happen to be the
most visible agency in every community.

One social agency funded by federal funds has been
in turmoil for the last three years over which personnel
should sign specific forms.   And this kind of nonsense is
being encouraged by those who talk about mass participation
on the part of all the people.   It is kind of a farce, a tra-
vesty really, to suggest that suddenly we are going to have
new ways of doing things; suddenly we are going to solve all
the problems by getting everybody together in a great town
meeting and deciding what we ought to do.   I indeed get very
much distressed and sometimes I even get a little angry at
all those folks who suggest that just any group of people can
get together and decide what and how schools ought to teach.

For those who believe in mass participation by those who
lack necessary expertise, I would suggest they follow this
principle when they need medical treatment. They should go
out on the street corner, collar the first ten people they
see and ask that group to diagnose and prognose their physical ills.

Although I hardly concur with the street corner ama-
teur running the schools, it is equally distressing that there
are so-called educational leaders who spend their time de-
fending the status quo rather than seeking new horizons.
Also, our problem has been that we have been engaged in
seeking too many simple answers to complex problems. For
example, today the fad is to promote contract performance,
accountability, vouchers, and alternative schools as solutions
to urban school problems. Many of these ideas are old
thoughts with new labels.

One other suggestion for combating our urban school
problems which has been popular is community control. I
do not want to imply that I have little faith in this suggestion; however, what has happened up to the present has been
very discouraging. Instead of communities focusing on the
legitimate needs of children, they have been in the midst of
an internal power struggle to capture and control the local
school board. It is interesting to note that in many instances
those people involved in the power struggle have received
more attention than the needs of the children in the school
district.

Our schools' first requisite is the need for trained
teachers in the classroom. Although our staffs today have
a far more liberal education than teachers prepared two or
three decades ago, I regret to say they are inadequately
trained for the challenge which face them in our urban
schools. I think we ought to get away from the notion that
training is not respectable. Our teachers need both a broad,
liberal background and professional training. Techniques of
teaching cannot be ignored.

Another facet of personnel which is of deep concern
to me is staff assignments and designations. We have many
personnel classifications in our school system. Hopefully,
all these specialists are facilitating the learning process. If
they are not accomplishing or contributing to this objective,
we are indeed wasting tax dollars. Specialists in such areas
as nutrition, social work, and psychology are all needed in

our schools, but I cannot ignore the fact that the business of
learning is the primary purpose of our schools.

All is not well with primary and elementary education, but our high school is probably the most archaic unit
in our educational structure.   The high school curriculum is
out-dated, vocational training is decades behind the real world
of work, and our attitudes toward school subjects do not
promote the well-being of our diversified student population.

In conclusion, I would simply like to reaffirm what
James B. Conant said: that we have social dynamite present
among our young people.   I believe the dynamite is accumu-
lating and its explosiveness is increasing in cities across the
country.   In some instances, we already have had explosions.
It is about time that we move one step ahead of those explosions and plan programs which will assist the disadvantaged
and underprivileged people of our cities.

12. ALTERNATIVES FOR URBAN SCHOOL REFORM

by Mario D. Fantini

At the very beginning of this paper, let me say that
I have been an urban teacher, and I know what it is like to
be inside the educational system trying to make it work. I
have also been an educational administrator. More recently
I have experienced what it is like to look at the educational
system from the outside: as a parent, an educational consumer, and as a critic, if you will. My purpose in review-
ing current educational practices is not to "blast" the public
schools but to suggest realistic, constructive suggestions
which can lead to the reform of our schools, especially the
schools of urban America.

My thesis is that the educational system, in which
you and I find ourselves captive, forged as it was during the
19th century, is inadequate for the America of the 1970's
and handicaps those inside of it trying to make it work.
This outdated structure had forced us into a pattern of reform which is simply "add on" in nature. We have added
on layers such as vocational education, special education,
early childhood education, and compensatory education. But
the basic public school structure right now is so ponderous
that it is incapable of serving effectively increased numbers
of educational consumers. Although the educational establishment is presently probably serving about 60 or 70 percent of
the population, there is emerging a critical mass of discon-
tented educational consumers who are looking at the school
in survival terms. They are requesting quality education,
but they believe they are simply receiving a second-rate product. Consequently, in an open society like ours, when an
institution as basic as the school reaches a plateau and cannot provide necessary services to the consumer, obviously
a fundamental question is raised concerning the process for
bringing about a reconstruction of that institution, at least
for those who are discontent.

I am interested in the process for bringing about the
necessary reform as well as the direction of the reforms

115

themselves.   We have attempted several types.   A review
and assessment of these may be useful.   Clearly our piecemeal approach to the educational problems are simply not
working.   A broader view of the overall problem is needed.
For example, for years now we have instituted crash program for rehabilitative dropouts, slow readers, the disadvantaged, and the gifted to adjust to the standard educational
process.   However, we have not directed our energies to the
real heart of our problem--the institution itself, its organi-
zational structure, and its over-all mode of operation.

       A range of innovations in public education has left the
basic system unchanged.   They have served to strengthen the
existing educational process enabling the system to serve
better those it has always served best.   The heart of the
present crisis in public education is the realization that the
system has failed a major segment of the population.   In a
pluralistic society this is serious business, indeed.   This
failure was the most intractable crisis all along, but it did
not come to full public awareness until the nation took official
cognizance of poverty amidst affluence and until the nonwhite
fourth of society's economic underclass began to assert its
civil rights and demand a full share in political and economic opportunity.

       A response to the present crisis is the intervention
of compensatory education.   It attempts to overcome short-
comings and is designed to raise pupils' academic achievement.   It characterizes such efforts as the Great Cities
School Improvement Programs (supported by the Ford Foundation), Title I of the Elementary and Secondary Education
Act, and New York City's early Higher Horizons Program
and more recent More Effective Schools Program.   Compensatory education seeks to attack a spectrum of defects in the
learner-verbal retardation, lack of motivation, and experi-
ential and sensory deprivation that presumably prevent his
participation in the learning process.   In addition to graft-
ing extra education onto the regular school experience, pro-
ponents of compensation have attempted to nip deficiencies in
the bud through pre-school programs like Project Headstart.

       For the most part, however, compensatory education
is a prescription that deals with symptoms.   It offers
strengthened doses of prescriptions that have been ineffective
before--more trips, more remedial reading, etc.   It is
essentially an additive, or "band-aid" approach that works by
augmenting and strengthening existing programs.

The compensatory approach is viewed with increasing distrust by the parents of academic failures both because the techniques are not achieving their goals, and because these parents are rejecting the premise that the fault lies with their children. Doubts are also beginning to rise among educational strategists who are disappointed by the failure of incremental inputs to the existing system to make a substantial difference. In his 1970 education message, President Nixon rendered a devasting verdict on compensatory education:

> We now spend more than $1 billion a year for educational programs run under Title 1 of the Elementary and Secondary Educational Act. Most of these have stressed the teaching of reading, but before-and-after tests suggest that only 19% of the children in such programs improve their reading significantly; 13% appear to fall behind more than expected; and more than two-thirds of the children remain unaffected--that is, they continue to fall behind. In our Headstart program, where so much hope is invested, we find that youngsters enrolled only for the summer achieve almost no gains, and the gains of those in the program for a full year are matched by their non-Headstart classmates from similarly poor backgrounds.

Another approach of intervention is desegregation. Since the 1954 Supreme Court decision, considerable effort toward desegregation has been based on the assumption that black pupils' achievement is enhanced in a racially balanced school environment.

In most urban settings, desegregation has proved elusive, if not impossible. The failure to achieve desegregation to any significant extent was due first to massive white resistance and racism. Now it is even less likely to occur in our lifetimes because of the growing concentration in the inner city of black and other nonwhite minorities. The only possible plans for achieving desegregation in many large cities are at the option of the white majority. The new focus of racial-minority parents is on power and control over the schools their children attend.

The implications for public education is greater participation by blacks in control over predominantly black schools. This is rather different from the "separate but equal" doc-

trine, since some "black power" philosophers reason that
when blacks achieve quality education under their own aegis,
they will then be prepared to connect (desegregate) with the
white society on a basis of parity instead of deficiency.   A
good school then would be defined not by the kind of children
who attend it, but by the quality of the education it offers.
In short, they seek connection as equals.

The goals of desegregation, therefore, must not be
abandoned but broadened to restore cultural diversity as a
value.   That is, we must reaffirm our commitment to connect with one another as human beings.   We must recognize
that viewing diversity and differences as assets rather than
unfortunate barriers to homogeneity has as positive an effect
on human growth and development as the teaching of academic skills.   All of which is to suggest that militant black
demands for participation in control of public institutions
serving predominantly black learners is actually a means of
greater connection to society, precisely opposite from the
connotations of separatism usually associated with "black
power. "

An indigenous participatory movement aimed at re-
forming urban school systems is decentralization.   Participation under this form comes through, in part, as shared
decision making: the educational consumers--in this case, the
parents and community residents--have anywhere from an
advisory to an equal voice with those who are operating the
existing educational system.   The difference between administrative decentralization, which is established practice in
many large school districts, and political decentralization
(governance) is that the latter creates a new public relationship between communities and their public schools, a relationship in which there is a basic redistribution of authority
and responsibility.   Under political decentralization in big
city systems (New York, Detroit), parents and community
residents share certain decisions with a central school board.
The same is true with the superintendent of schools, teachers' and/or supervisors' association, and so on.

Decentralization is a federation of local school boards,
each with limited authority over a portion of the total school
system.   Under this scheme, there would be a city-wide
school system with a central school authority which may have
final veto power over most decisions which local boards could
make, or which can impose sanctions on local districts
through appeals to the state.   Procedures governing recruit-

ment, selection, transfer, and tenure of personnel; budget;
maintenance; and curriculum must be worked out together.
Usually each group must compromise to achieve a consensus.
These consensus procedures become the new ground rules for
making decentralization work.

Community control, in its purest form, shifts to a
local school board the bulk of the authority necessary for
governing schools.   Under maximum community control, a
locality may not share decision making with a central school
board; the local board may be independent of the central
board and assume the same status as any other school district in the state.   Since education is a state function, the
local district shares authority with the state and is subjected
to state regulation.   There is, therefore, no absolute control
as such.   However, under community control, sections of
city schools--usually in the heart of the city--secede from
the larger school system to become an independent school
district.   As an independent district the community is free
to recruit, hire, transfer and release personnel--the same
way as, for example, a Scarsdale or a Newton can.

Other approaches to quality education are an escape
into a parallel system.   Such approaches assume that if the
poor (or others) cannot reform public education, the system
is meaningless to the poor and they should be afforded options to it.

The voucher approach serves as an escape and has to
be rated high in both significance and public popularity.   The
voucher idea attempts to increase the purchasing power for
the poor by placing in their hands a new type of educational
purchasing power.   This is accomplished by issuing to parents a "voucher" (certificate) worth a given amount of money
to be used as full or partial tuition payment at a school,
private or public, of the parent's choice.   While the voucher
proposals being advanced by various agencies tend to include
the public school among the alternatives from which a citizen
may choose, in actuality, the plan is skewed in the direction
of non-public school options.

The voucher concept can therefore be viewed as having
either an external or internal emphasis.   The externally oriented voucher system emphasizes access to alternative schools
outside public school systems.   The internally oriented
voucher plan views access to alternatives existing within the
framework of public school systems.   Both plans rely on in-

creased consumer interest in alternative forms of education
and in their right of choice.

Counter to the public schools is the private schools.
A few privately managed schools have been established in
urban ghettoes, and several others are in the planning stage.
Precedents for such a school exist in southern Freedom
Schools.   Some northern counterparts include Harlem's Academies of Transition and the New School in Boston's Roxbury
section.   The Urban League-sponsored Street Academies and
Harlem Prep are reporting success with the so-called hard-
core rejects from the public school system.

Non-public schools have advantages: they do not have
to deal with distant and entrenched bureaucracies, with school
boards unfamiliar with their particular needs, or with teachers' unions.   They are free to hire teachers from a variety
of personnel pools and to sidestep rigid credential procedures.
They may even abandon such practices as tenure, and retain,
promote, or discharge teachers purely on the grounds of
merit and performance.   If the schools are governed by boards
with a substantial representation of their pupils' parents, they
are likely to be more responsive to the children's needs and
thereby encourage better rapport and partnership between the
home and the school.   In the most general sense, they afford the poor the choice that is open to many middle-class
parents: to educate their children elsewhere if they are dis-
satisfied with the performance of the public schools.   And if
enough private schools are available, the pattern ushers in an
entrepreneurial system in which parents can choose, cafeteria-
style, from a range of styles of education--Montessori, prep
school, Summerhill, and others.   This is the hope of the educational voucher experiments now being investigated by the
Office of Economic Opportunity.

Carried to its logical conclusion, however, the paral-
lel-school approach would reduce the scope of public education, if not dispense with it altogether.   The establishment of
private schools sufficient to handle significant numbers of
poor children would require public support and, in effect, establish a private system of publicly-supported schools.   Mid-
dle-income parents would demand similar privileges.   For
financial and political reasons alone, the voucher approach is
unlikely to become widespread in the foreseeable future;
moreover, the scheme would founder on political, if not constitutional grounds.   Finally, since private schools are not
subjected to public control, there would be no guarantee that

some private education might not be organized by special interest groups for ends inimical to a free and open society.
Support of such enterprises at public expense would be in-
tolerable.

These arguments are, of course, no reason to dis-
courage programs that enable more low-income pupils to attend private schools.   Private schools could serve a valuable
yardstick function if they were run under conditions that sim-
ulated the resources and inputs of public education--particu-
larly comparable per-capita expenditures, and admission
policies that would embrace a range of low-income pupils,
including the "disruptive. " But that is the limit of their use-
fulness as an alternative to improved public education, for
they could never serve the majority of the children of the
poor.

Is there any way of dealing with the dilemma? We
certainly have learned some lessons.   The trick will be to
find a proposed reform that is realistic; it must make contact with the current forces, including the political nature of
public schools at this time.   These are no guarantees for
success.

These lessons have to become the ground rules for
any new reform proposal, that it:

1.   demonstrate adherence to a COMPREHENSIVE
SET OF EDUCATIONAL OBJECTIVES--not particular ones.
Proposals cannot, for example, emphasize only emotional
growth at the expense of intellectual development.   The converse is also true.   Comprehensive educational objectives
deal with work careers, citizenship, talent development, intellectual and emotional growth, problem solving, critical
thinking, and the like.
2.   does not SUBSTANTIALLY INCREASE THE PER
STUDENT EXPENDITURE from that of established programs.
To advance an idea which doubles or triples the budget will
at best place the proposal in the ideal, but not practical,
category.   Further, an important factor for reformers to
bear in mind is that the new arena will deal with wiser use
of OLD money, not the quest for add-on money.
3.   does not ADVOCATE ANY FORM OF EXCLU-
SIVITY--racial, religious, or economic.   Solutions cannot
deny equal access to any particular individual or group.
4.   is not SUPER-IMPOSED.   The days of a small
group planning FOR or doing TO others are fading out.

5.   respect the RIGHTS OF ALL CONCERNED
PARTIES AND APPLY TO EVERYONE--it cannot appear to
serve the interests of one group only.   Thus, for instance,
if decentralization plans of urban schools systems are inter-
preted to serve only minority communities, then the majority
community may very well oppose such efforts.
6.   does not claim a SINGLE ACROSS-THE-BOARD
MODEL ANSWER, no blanket panacea to the educational
problem.   Attempts at uniform solutions are almost never
successful.
7.   advocate a PROCESS OF CHANGE WHICH IS
DEMOCRATIC and it maximizes individual decision-making.
Participation by the individual in the decisions which affect
his life is basic to comprehensive support. *

    In light of this, we propose our plan--Public Schools
of Choice, an approach that retains the overall conception of
public education and provides educational options that hereto-
fore were available only outside the public school system,
and makes them available through voluntary choice by the
consumer.

    A Public Schools of Choice system establishes a
broader conception of public education for today's society,
one that opens up decision-making opportunities for all parties who have intrinsic interest in the quality of schooling.
It responds to the queries: why can a public school not develop alternative forms of education within its own framework?   Why cannot the educational process which we now
have be but one legitimate means for achieving our educational objectives?   Why can teachers whose teaching styles
lead to a different educational process not be allowed to develop an alternative by choice?   Why can't those students
and parents who prefer the option developed by teacher select it by choice?

    Those teachers, students and parents who prefer the
standard process have a right to it.   Those teachers, students and parents who prefer options should also have their
right.

    Such a plan can begin at any school, at any grade,

---

*Fantini, Mario D.   "Public Schools of Choice and the Plu-
rality of Publics, " Educational Leadership, vol. 28, no. 6,
March 1971.
Also from this article are the eight "Options" detailed below.

almost immediately.   For example, if a school has four first
grades, why can't three be traditional and one open?   All
that is necessary is that of the four first grade teachers, one
has the style, disposition and willingness to offer an option,
say "open classroom. "   Parent meetings can be held to provide basic information on the open classroom.   Those parents
who wish to explore this further can meet again with the interested teacher and administration.   After a series of ses-
sions, it is possible that, without additional costs, parents,
student and teacher will have chosen another legitimate option.   Individualization would occur by matching teacher-style
and learning environment with learner style.   At the high
school level, teachers and students may conceptualize an alternative "school within a school" or a "mini school" based
on the principle of multi-cultural education.

In Philadelphia, an alternative public school was established around the concept of a school without walls on
which the city became the classroom.   This school without
walls (Parkway Program) was not imposed on any teachers,
students or parents, but became a form of education for
which these parties were attracted by choice.

A school or school system could develop a range of
educational options:

Option 1.   Traditional: The school is graded and
emphasizes the acquisition of basic skills, i. e., reading,
writing, and mathematics, by cognitive methods.   The basic
learning unit is the classroom, manned by one or more
teachers who direct and instruct in their tasks.   Students
are encouraged to adapt to the style of the school.   Youngsters with diagnosed learning handicaps participate in remedial programs.   The educational and fiscal policy of this
school is determined entirely by the Central Board of Education.

Option 2.   Open and Non-Graded: This school re-
sembles the primary schools and Leicestershire Infant
Schools of Britain.   The "school" is divided into learning
"areas, " each containing many constructional and manipulative materials.   Youngsters work individually or in small
groups on various specialized learning projects, with the
teachers acting as facilitators, rather than managers. Many
activities occur outside the school building.

Option 3.   Career-Oriented: This school fosters

learning by experience. The school is responsible for identifying individual talents and prescribing suitable experiences
for their nourishment. Various learning and teaching styles
are operational here, and concrete performance is deemed
as important as theoretical proficiency. This program is
geared toward the work world.

Option 4. Automated: The programs at this school
utilize technological devices. Computers are used for diag-
nosis of the students' needs and abilities, and subsequent instruction. The library contains banks of tape recordings
and "talking, " "listening, " and manipulative carrels which
can be student-operated. Closed circuit television is offered
in this school, as well as Nova-type retrieval systems for
student-teacher conferences on individual learning problems.

Option 5. Total Community School: This school
operates on a 12- to 14-hour basis for at least six days a
week all year. Adults and children participate in educational
and civic programs. The facility provides services for
health, legal aid, and employment. Paraprofessionals or
community teachers assist in every phase of the regular
school program, and the school is controlled by a board of
community representatives. This board hires the two chief
administrators, one of whom directs all other activities in
the school. More than a school, this institution is a community center.

Option 6. Montessori: Students move at their own
pace and are largely self-directed. The learning areas are
rich with creative selection. The teacher functions within a
specifically defined methodology, but she is a guide, not a
director. The development of sensory perception is empha-
sized in Montessori classrooms.

Option 7. Multi-Culture School: Named for the model
in San Francisco, this school is defined by its ethnic heter-
ogeneity. As many as five ethnic groups may be equally
represented, and part of each day separates these groups for
homogeneous learning. These classes are concerned with the
language, customs, history, and heritage of the respective
group. Several times per week one group shares an aspect
of its culture with the other students. Diversity is the outstanding value here, and its curriculum is humanistic in
content. Questions of group identity, inter-group identity,
power, and individual identity are discussed at that optional
school. It is governed by a policy board, comprised of

equal numbers of parents and teachers, which is only tangentially responsible to the central board of education.

Option 8. Performance Contract School: Educational consumers may want to subcontract with an educational firm to operate one of its public schools. In Gary, Indiana, Behavioral Research Laboratories is operating the Banneker Elementary School. Under a contract with the public schools, the contract contains a money-back guarantee that the children in the school will achieve a certain set of educational objectives, i.e., reading at grade level. The Banneker program makes wide use of individualized reading materials developed by the company.

At present, the Berkeley Unified School District in California has an alternative schools plan which offers over 20 educational options directly to parents, students, teachers and administrators.

What we are suggesting is an "internal voucher" system, educational alternatives within the framework of public education. Such a plan would, we believe, receive internal professional support and start to meet the complex core of public demands.

The proposals would strengthen the concept of public education in the United States, not attempt to weaken or destroy it. As a type of supply and demand model, the internal voucher would stimulate development by continuously offering new and better ways of educating children without scrapping the best of the old. A Public School of Choice educational system would be judged by results. It would be, in essence, a performance model.

Public schools would also protect the public from sectarian interests based on exclusivity. Under a Public Schools of Choice system, there would be no chance for a "Nazi School" to be sanctioned.

Public schools have the manpower and the mechanism to develop an internal voucher framework immediately. Presently the manpower is directed at trying to improve the one standard alternative, not in the development of further alternatives. Access to parent and community education and involvement is enhanced in a public school of choice system. Unless basic information about alternatives reaches students and parents, it will be difficult for an internal voucher plan to succeed. But public schools have the means for contacting students and parents on this new program of options.

Public education in America has evolved a common set of educational objectives but has thus far relied on one monolithic means for achieving them. Given our diversity and the individual right of choice in our society, it is possible that the participation movement will lead beyond decentralization and community control and toward public schools of choice.

13. URBAN EDUCATION: BEGINNING OR END OF AN ERA?

by Philip D. Vairo

When one views the broad range of urban problems--from pollution, growth of crime, unemployment, racial and economic segregation, and poor housing conditions to insufficient revenues, it is difficult to single out any particular one as the source of our urban difficulties. Our inability to find ways to solve the problems which face our cities is having serious economic and social consequences.

Harry N. Rivlin, who is dean of the School of Education at Fordham University, recently stated that "education in the United States is pretty good--and that's the trouble. Pretty good just is not good enough in times of enormous potential and tremendous problems." It has been frequently pointed out that the greatest assets that our cities have are its people. The people of our cities, especially the urban poor, need to be consulted in public school governance. If there is to be an urban renaissance in the decade ahead, the poor will need to play an active rather than passive role in developing new patterns in urban education. It is ironic that although we are in the midst of exploring the validity of turning federal funds over to local governments, on the assumption that these governments best understand local needs, we hesitate to give the urban poor a real voice in their schools. President Nixon on several occasions has spoken of revenue sharing as a partnership between the federal, state, and local government. The tragedy is that the urban poor have never enjoyed the privilege of participating in the affairs of the city, especially in the education of their children. The fact is that the poor today want and indeed have a right to participate in educational policy-making.

In the United States, local control of education has always been considered a virtue, but the moment the urban poor sought to play a role in determining educational policy, many questions were raised about their competency. The most often cited example is that the poor do not have the qualifications for intelligent school governance. However, the critics neglect to mention that the poor are eligible to vote for United States Senators and the President of the United States.   For much too long we have relied on the so-called suburban experts to solve the problems of the poor.   Some of the funds allocated for consulting services should be detoured to the poor to determine their own destiny.   Of course, guidelines must be carefully drawn that delineate duties, responsibilities, as well as the role, scope and mission of the community consultants.   The poor want and have a right to be heard on educational matters which will affect their children.   They are going to have a voice in public education, one way or another.

        The question of community governance is not limited solely to the educational establishment.   Congressman Herman Badillo of New York City has proposed building community hospitals run by community boards.   So far, Congressman Badillo has made little progress in achieving his goal.   He has criticized community hospital advisory committees for the very same reasons that many have criticized similar committees established to serve urban schools.   Badillo pointed out that community advisory boards simply do not have the power to make decisions concerning the real issues which face hospitals and patients in our urban ghettos.   The community must have more than simply an advisory role in their public schools, hospitals, and other human service agencies.

        The urban poor can provide a degree of relevance for teacher education programs as well as for the elementary and secondary school curriculum by helping the students and the faculty to develop insights into the pressing social, political, and educational problems of today.   Colleges of education must include the urban poor in their deliberations.   The urban poor can serve as resource people to assist teachers and those who train teachers to understand and work effectively in the big city ghettos.   It is about time that we consult the poor about programs that will involve them.   Opportunities must be provided for the urban poor to qualify for paraprofessional and professional positions through existing programs offered at universities and colleges.   Specially designed career ladder programs should also be implemented in our colleges and universities.

        The urban poor's voice in school governance must also include an opportunity to participate in the selection of

senior administrative personnel. What is difficult to justify
is the deep chasm between the urban poor and decision-making school personnel who should presumably be able to work
together for the betterment of the community. Relations between the poor and school administrators are frequently non-
existent. Channels of communication must not only be open
but must serve as viable vehicles for the improvement of
school-community relationships. The urban poor upon ob-
taining college training must be encouraged to continue to
serve the community in which they and their parents now live.
We cannot rely solely on teachers who come from middle-
class backgrounds, which milieu shielded them from the
problems of the urban ghetto, to teach the urban poor. We
need the assistance of those persons who are alert to the
needs and pressures of minority groups. First-hand life experiences plus realistic professional preparation are the in-
gredients so desperately needed to understand the problems
of the poor. Without real-life experiences in the ghetto, even
the best-intentioned faculty member or administrator may
simply not be sensitive to the frustrations and despair of the
urban poor.

We shall indeed be wasting a rare opportunity if we
do no more than give lip service to the urban poor. The
number of urban poor in our cities is multiplying rapidly.
In 1980, eighty-five percent of all Americans will live in
metropolitan areas, and a large number of these inhabitants
will be economically and culturally underprivileged.

Although the problems of our cities have been with us
for decades, surprisingly, American urban universities, public and private, have not shown as much concern with urban
education and urban problems as the so-called "cow" colleges did when rural education was a major problem. Only
recently, and at best during the last decade or so, have
urban institutions become sensitive to their location and developed some obligation to serve the city and its people.

Examining the history of the main campus of any state
university system, one will note that departments of rural
sociology, rural education, rural economics, agriculture and
many related areas were established many decades ago and
are still presently operational. Furthermore, these institutions established colleges of agriculture and agricultural ex-
tension centers, and gave special attention to recruiting and
preparing teachers for rural schools.

On the other hand, programs in urban education and urban studies are newcomers to higher education as is the publicly supported urban university. Doctoral studies in urban education have only emerged during the past two or three years. The idea of establishing an urban state university campus in many large cities has finally taken hold in the United States. For example, we now have the Chicago Circle Campus of the University of Illinois, the University of Missouri at St. Louis and at Kansas City, the University of Wisconsin at Milwaukee, and Louisiana State University at New Orleans. Although these institutions have been established in our large cities, it has been pointed out that there is a need for careful review of the appropriations made to urban universities. There are those who believe that the distribution of funds by some state legislatures continually shortchanges the urban campuses at the expense of the established state university. After all it is the established campus that usually has the prestigious football team, advanced graduate degree programs, distinguished scholars, and impressive physical plant.

Another concern is how we can best attain racial integration in our schools--through busing, low and middle income housing developments in suburbia, or whatever. William McClure, director of educational research at the University of Illinois, recently testified in U. S. District Court in Richmond, Virginia that busing a child out of his school area could result in disorientation, and that his parents would no longer be interested in the neighborhood school. Whether there is validity to this position is a wide-open question. However, it seems that instead of addressing ourselves to the real issues which face our nation and particularly our cities, we are expending our energy and money on an issue which is in essence peripheral. It is about time that open housing is made a reality to all Americans. Preferential treatment of middle-class whites at the expense of minorities cannot continue to exist. We need to increase opportunities for low-skilled workers to earn living wages so that they will be able to improve their standard of living and afford decent housing for their families. Economic as well as racial segregation must be eliminated. Dirty, dilapidated tenements cannot continue to house the urban poor. Rigid enforcement of housing codes, elimination of slum landlords, and well-planned urban renewal projects are needed.

For those citizens who oppose busing I ask: are you prepared to accept not only in principle but in practice open

housing in your community? What steps will be taken in
your neighborhood to promote and spread the spirit of good
will toward all men?   What concerted efforts to integrate the
schools, if any, have been made in your neighborhood and
city prior to recent court decisions?   It is indeed regrettable
that we cannot take the initiative where social justice war-
rants rather than wait for the courts to decide for us.

The Plessy v. Ferguson decision in 1896 upheld the
constitutional validity of separate but equal facilities.   It is
difficult to understand how this nation stood by and graciously
accepted the "separate but equal" principle during the very
period of our history in which our nation fought two world
wars in the name of democracy.   There is little doubt that
now is the time for all of us to re-examine America's housing policies--home purchases, apartment rentals, cooperative
ownership, and condominiums.   If the federal government can
act in the name of the common good to control wages and
prices, it should without hesitation develop a national housing
plan equitable to all men.

Furthermore, it is also about time that our present
system of financing public education through assessed property value be examined by the courts.   Children of the poor
cannot continue to be penalized because their parents are
poor.   The per pupil expenditure in our school districts must
be equalized, keeping in mind such factors as cost of living
and other local differences.   Also, we cannot continue to rely
solely on property taxes to support education.   The burden
of property taxation on our lower middle class is another in-
equity.   New sources of revenue must be found.

One area which needs our immediate attention lies in
the improvements of teaching reading.   We need smaller
classes in the first four grades of school, classes with no
more than ten students, with each individual getting a maximum of attention.   Reducing the class size in the primary
grades need not mean that cities would have to increase their
educational budgets twofold.   This end can be accomplished,
if the city's finances so require, by increasing the class size
in the junior and senior high schools.   Ideally, a decrease in
the teacher-pupil ratio for all grade levels should be the
goal, but urban revenues are limited.   If our elementary
school pupils cannot read, we need no longer worry about
secondary education for them.   Drastic action is warranted
one way or another! We can no longer tolerate the present
situation where in some of our cities over 50 percent of

ghetto students are not reading at grade level. We are indeed opening the door to frustration, delinquency, and dropping-out. If the school is going to be a place which attracts students, our young people are going to need the essential tool of success--reading.

Men should be encouraged to teach on the primary level, especially in low income urban areas. The security and positive image portrayed by the male teacher in the child's formative years should not be minimized. Lee J. Cronbach, a renowned psychologist, almost two decades ago pointed out that a balanced elementary school faculty needs a variety of personalities as well as men on its staff. During the past ten years the author has interviewed scores of elementary school principals from New York, North Carolina, New Jersey, and Tennessee, and only a few recalled males teaching in the primary grades. It was pointed out that the male teacher's duration, however, was shortlived. He either left the profession or went into school administration.

It is regrettable that so many teachers at all school levels find themselves moving into educational administration as a means to increase their salaries. We would not think of forcing a skilled surgeon to become a hospital administrator in order to advance economically, yet we do just that in our schools. Why not pay a qualified teacher a salary comparable to a school administrator? After all, the teacher is where it counts--the classroom. Urban schools need first-rate teachers.

What happens to the student after he completes his schooling or leaves school is another concern which should not be overlooked. Today in a world of changing dimensions, numerous factors exist in our economy that contribute to a confusing pattern of job possibilities. The selection of an occupation not only may determine whether the student will be employed or unemployed, successful or unsuccessful, but will indeed influence almost every aspect of his life. The urban poor have complained about their inability to gain fruitful employment in the world of work. Because occupational choices are increasingly being made in the school house remote from many of the realities of the world of work, it is imperative that a quality program in career development be established. It is incumbent upon the school to present a realistic appraisal of occupations with up-to-date future projections, even though it is difficult to foretell the job market needs of the 1980's. Students should be made aware of career ladder opportunities as well as the realities and myths of vertical mobility. Sidney P. Marland, Jr., United States Commissioner of Education, recently pointed out that career education could very well begin as early as the primary grades.

If we are going to have a new era in urban education, our children must be as happy to return to school in September as they are anxious to leave in June. It is sad that our children sing songs in June and moan in September. Perhaps in the 1970's we can reverse this pattern.

The urban poor want quality education now. Hoy, Sí; Mañana, No!

Epilogue

THE UNHEAVENLY CITY IN WESTERN LITERATURE

by Thomas R. Preston

The ancient Greek playwright, Aeschylus, presents in
The Eumenides the image of a man caught between two con-
flicting laws.   Following the divine law to avenge his father's
murder, Orestes kills his mother and thereby breaks the law
forbidding the murder of parents.   The dilemma is solved by
the goddess Athena.

> Summon the city, herald, and proclaim the cause;
> Let the Turrhenian trumpet, filled with mortal breath,
> Crack the broad heaven, and shake Athens with its voice.
> And while the council-chamber fills, let citizens
> And jurors all in silence recognize this court
> Which I ordain today in perpetuity,
> That now and always justice may be well discerned.
> [Philip Vellacott translation.]

This solution to Orestes' dilemma is strikingly pro-urban.
Aeschylus associates the city of Athens with the goddess
Athena, after whom the city indeed is named, and he enun-
ciates the idea that law and justice are specifically urban
virtues, an idea we maintain to this day by distinguishing between justice and such deviations as "frontier justice" and
"kangaroo courts."   Aeschylus' urban bias reflects the whole
of ancient Greek culture, which gloried in the city-state and
believed, with Aristotle, that in the city man developed the
moral, intellectual, and political virtues that fulfilled his
nature.   It is impossible to recall ancient Greek literature
even vaguely without thinking of Plato's Republic and of the
urban ethos in plays like Antigone and Oedipus Rex.   We
remember in the Iliad Homer's sadness that Troy must fall,
Troy whose repeated epithets are the "city of wide streets"
and the "city of women with long, trailing gowns."

With the fall of ancient Greece, western literature

134

shifted from an urban to a rural bias, and that rural bias re-
mained almost unchallenged until very recent times. The
great empire of Rome that succeeded ancient Greece was cel-
ebrated, for example, in Vergil's Aeneid, but the eternal city
itself received constant literary attack, arousing the antipathy
of writers as different as Horace and Juvenal. One of the
great paradoxes of Western civilization is that, from the time
of the ancient Greeks, western man has been urbanizing, but
in his literature he has turned his back on the city and glori-
fied the country.

In large part this rural bias has expressed itself
through the pastoral tradition which, ironically, developed in
ancient Greece and is the product of an urbane, sophisticated
sensibility. The pastoral impulse seeks to identify and to
define, beneath the complexities of human life, those elements
informing the ideal state of human existence in which man
enjoys perfect physical and moral harmony. The pastoral
impulse, whether it is embodied in the specific literary form
called the pastoral or in some other form like the elegy, ex-
plores that ideal state in terms of an idealized rural setting.
The precedent for this approach is, of course, set by the
classical image of the Golden Age, but the strongest influence
sustaining it is probably the biblical image of the Garden of
Eden. Both images, however, remind man that the ideal
state of physical and moral harmony once existed in some
pre-historic, pre-urban past.

Under the spell of these images western literature has
been filled with idealized countrysides where elegant sheep
graze on the greenest of grass and shepherd-swains dance,
sing, hold piping contests, make love, and die in the odor of
roses. The image of the country or garden as a place of
evil does, of course, exist, as Spenser's Bower of Bliss in
the Faerie Queene reminds us, but some of the great and
most influential works of western literature fall into the pastoral tradition: Vergil's Georgics, Spenser's Shepeardes
Calender, Sidney's Arcadia, Guarini's Il Pastor Fido, Mar-
vell's garden poetry, Milton's "Lycidas," Gray's "Elegy,"
Tennyson's "In Memoriam," Arnold's "Thyrsis." It is no
accident that many of today's young people voice their dis-
satisfaction with modern society by wearing flowers and urg-
ing "flower power" or by attempting to form rural communes.
They are simply following the pastoral tradition, attempting
to "realize" its idealized life style.

As the attempt of the young people suggests, one of

the effects of the pastoral tradition in western literature has
been to cause a confusion of the ideal and the real country,
a confusion of the symbolic rural setting with the values
symbolized by that setting.   Because a close enough surface
correspondence exists between the rural symbols of the ideal
country and rural aspects of the real country, the western
mind has tended, if not to identify the two completely, at
least to think that the values symbolized in the pastoral tradition can be more nearly achieved in the real country than
in the city.   This formula of opposing the country to the city
has been another major way western literature has expressed
its rural bias.   The opposition between the country and the
city becomes one in which the city is damned and rejected
while the country is praised and projected as a refuge against
the evils of the city.   Both biblical precedent and cultural
myths, ironically, warrant the use of urban settings to project the ideal of physical and moral harmony.   As Harvey
Cox has noted in his Secular City, the Bible, while it places
man in a garden in the first book of Scripture, nevertheless
envisions him in a city in the last book, St. John's Reve-
lation.

> And there came unto me one of the seven angels ...
> saying, Come hither, I will shew thee the bride, the
> Lamb's wife.   And he ... shewed me that great city,
> the holy Jerusalem, descending out of heaven from
> God, having the glory of God: and her light was like
> unto a stone most precious, even like a jasper stone,
> clear as crystal; and had a wall great and high, and
> had twelve gates....   And the city lieth four-square,
> and the length is as large as the breadth....   And the
> building of the wall of it was jasper: and the city was
> pure gold, like unto clear glass.   And the foundations
> of the wall of the city were garnished with all manner
> of precious stones.   [Revelation 21:9-20.]

The ideal state of physical and moral harmony are
thus in Scripture symbolized by both the country and the city,
so that on the ideal level, at least, the country and the city
are one.   Moreover, as Mircea Eliade has shown in Cosmos
and History, nearly all cultures share the myth that real
cities are copies of heavenly archetypes.   In Hebrew tradition
Jerusalem was supposedly graven on the palms of God's
hands, and in Psalm 87 David envisions Jerusalem as the
heavenly city realized on earth.

His foundation is in the holy mountains.
The Lord loveth the gates of Zion
More than all the dwellings of Jacob.
Glorious things are spoken of thee,
O city of God.   Selah.
I will make mention of Rahab and Babylon
    to them that know me:
Behold Philistia, and Tyre, with Ethopia;
This man was born there.
And of Zion it shall be said, This and that
    man was born in her:
And the highest himself shall establish her.
The Lord shall count, when he writeth up the people.
That this man was born there.   Selah.

Despite the biblical warrant and the cultural myths, however, the correspondence between the ideal and the real city, unlike that between the ideal and real country, has seemed remote, and western literature has tended to celebrate the city only as a desirable place that might have existed once--El Dorado, Atlantis--or that will come at the end of history--the New Jerusalem or St. Augustine's City of God.   The fusion of symbolic rural and urban settings occurs only outside history, in heaven, as Dante suggests in the Divine Comedy, where the heavenly city arises out of a rose.   The real city, supposedly first built by Cain the murderer, may be enticing, but it is also a place of evil and corruption--Babylon, Nineveh, Sodom, London, Paris, New York.   This image of the city as a place to seduce the body and soul has overshadowed the very virtues western literature admits the city fosters: commerce, trade, literature, music, painting, sculpture, architecture, dance, exotic food, great varieties of people, and, above all, intellectual and social intercourse.

As stated above, in rejecting the city, western literature has assumed that the virtues of the country--even when it is admitted that the country has defects and that evil can exist there too--offer a better chance for achieving the ideal state of physical and moral harmony than do the virtues of the city with their long train of attendant vices.   Here is Horace "To Aristius Fuscus":

                              I praise the brooks
Flowing through the sweet countryside, its stones
        overgrown
With moss, its delightful groves.   Need I say more?

I begin to live, I reign, as soon as I've left
The very same things you people praise to the skies. . . .
I need plain bread now, much more than honeyed
    cakes.

If it's only proper to "live in accordance with
    nature"
And we must put our houses somewhere, do you know
    anywhere
Better than the country, naturally so well situated?
Where winters are warmer, and welcome winds can
    soothe
The Dog Star's fury or the Lion's impatient thrust,
When goaded to rage by the first hot rays of the sun,
Where fewer frustrating worries ravel our sleep.
Where the grass smells finer and shines more than
    African mosaics.

Is the water purer that pounds its way through the
    pipes
In the city than that which scampers and murmurs
    along
Our sloping streams?   [Smith Palmer Bovie transla-
                                              tion.]

Horace is echoed throughout western literature, even in
the literature of that most pro-urban era, the eighteenth century.   The typical pattern of the eighteenth-century novel,
for example, sets the hero or heroine on the road from the
country to the city and back again to the country.   One of
the great eighteenth-century English satirists of the city,
Tobias Smollett, has Matthew Bramble, the main character
in his Humphry Clinker, explain this retreat to the country
when he praises the Dennisons for following this pattern.
Dennison's friends raised objections to a country life, but
these objections were proved wrong

            . . . because they were chiefly founded upon the sup-
            position that he would be obliged to lead a life of ex-
            travagance and dissipation, which he and his con-
            sort equally detested, despised, and determined to
            avoid.   The objects he had in view were health of
            body, peace of mind, and the private satisfaction
            of domestic quiet, unallayed by actual want, and
            uninterrupted by the fears of indigence. . . .   He re-
            quired nothing but wholesome air, pure water, plain
            diet, convenient lodging, and decent apparel
                                              [Signet edition].

The rural virtues Matthew Bramble extols are intended to outweigh rural defects and to oppose urban vices. When we examine these urban vices as they are exhibited in such works as Horace's Epodes, Juvenal's powerful third satire "Against the City of Rome," or in the works of Smollett, Fielding, Dickens, Thackeray, Thoreau, Balzac, T. S. Eliot, the English Romantic poets, and a host of other writers, we can abstract them into the following list: noise, luxury, dissipation, role-playing, bigness, hypocrisy, adulterated food, trivial amusement, breakdown of social decorum, money seeking, air pollution, licentiousness, violence (both physical and moral). The rural virtues, extrapolated from rural defects, are summarized in Oliver Goldsmith's famous "De serted Village":

> I see the rural virtues....
> Contented toil, and hospitable care,
> And kind connubial tenderness, are there;
> And piety, with wishes placed above,
> And steady loyalty, and faithful love.
> [Modern Library edition.]

In the country, with such virtues, man can presumably escape what Wordsworth calls the "lonely rooms" and the "din of towns and cities" (from "Tintern Abbey"). Rejecting the city in favor of the country he can learn all he needs for physical and moral harmony:

> One impulse from a vernal wood
> May teach you more of man,
> Of moral evil and of good,
> Than all the sages can.
> [Wordsworth, "The Tables Turned."]

Paradoxically, however, beneath the rurally biased surface of western literature we find a potential urban bias. In the first place, the pastoral tradition assumes that entering the world of the pastoral is only a temporary retreat after which man returns to the real world of complexity. Recall Shakespeare's pastoral plays: at the end of A Midsummer Night's Dream, the Athenians return to Athens; at the end of As You Like It, all but Jaques abandon the forest of Arden; and at the end of The Tempest, Prospero breaks his wand and returns to his dukedom of Milan. Even in the opposed country-city tradition there is usually a recognition that most men must live in the city, but that from the country they can derive the strength to live there creatively.

The following memorable lines from Wordsworth's "Tintern Abbey" capture this underlying theme.

                              The beauteous forms,
          Through a long absence, have not been to me
          As is a landscape to a blind man's eye ...
                              I have owed to them,
          In hours of weariness, sensations sweet,
          Felt in the blood, and felt along the heart....
                              feelings too
          Of unremembered pleasure: such, perhaps,
          As have no slight or trivial influence
          On that best portion of a good man's life,
          His little, nameless, unremembered, acts
          Of kindness and of love.   Nor less, I trust,
          To them I may have owed another gift,
          Of aspect more sublime; that blessed mood
          In which the burthen of the mystery,
          In which the heavy and the weary weight
          Of all this unintelligble world,
          Is lightened.

In the second place, the majority of the writers have them-selves been city dwellers, and certainly they have infused into their rural settings the virtues associated with the city. Horace on his Sabine farm is <u>not</u> a farmer, but a cultivated, urbane gentleman enjoying with equally urbane friends the virtues of the country without the defects--without manual labor, vermin, rodents, beasts, dung, boors, and the absence of engaging intellectual and social intercourse.

     In effect, western literature has prized a balance of rural and urban virtues and has tried to project this balance by informing the rural setting, however real or idealized, with urban virtues.   In one sense, this practice has been an evasion of urban problems, for it has allowed western litera-ture to exploit urban virtues, vividly portray and denounce urban defects and vices, and then retreat to the apparent safety of the country.   Since World War II, however, a new approach can be discerned.   The process of urbanization has moved so rapidly and become so intensified that the country itself has been almost completely urbanized: it is rural now only in setting, and it is a question of how long the setting will remain.   Urban structures like the corporation are now in the country, and the urban style appears on rural tele-vision every night.

     Faced with this fact of almost total urbanization,

western literature has been forced to deal with the city instead of fleeing from it.   We can discover a return to the
ancient Greek idea that the city is the place where man de-
velops the moral, intellectual, and political virtues that
fulfill his nature.   I do not mean to imply that we are moving towards an idealization of the city.   On the contrary,
contemporary writers still focus on its defects and vices.
But now the city is being viewed positively, as a crucible in
which man is refined and perhaps gradually civilized.   The
city is "where the action is, " and it is being treated as the
matrix for humanizing the "barbarian within. "   A precedent
for this new urban concern is found in some nineteenth-cen-
tury novelists who, at first, seem anti-urban--Dostoevsky,
Dickens, Balzac.

        Albert Camus' The Plague, published in 1948, perhaps
points the new direction in contemporary western literature.
The city of Oran is projected at the beginning of the novel in
terms of its defects.

> Perhaps the easiest way of making a town's ac-
> quaintance is to ascertain how the people in it work,
> how they love, and how they die.   In our little
> town ... all three are done on much the same
> lines, with the same feverish yet casual air.   The
> truth is that everyone is bored, and devotes him-
> self to cultivating habits.   Our citizens work hard,
> but solely with the object of getting rich.   Their
> chief interest is in commerce, and their chief aim
> in life is, as they call it, 'doing business. '   Na-
> turally they don't eschew such simpler pleasures
> as love-making, sea-bathing, going to the pictures.
> But, very sensibly, they reserve these pastimes
> for Saturday afternoons and Sundays and employ the
> rest of the week in making money, as much as
> possible.   In the evening, on leaving the office,
> they forgather, at an hour that never varies, in
> the cafes, stroll the same boulevard, or take the
> air on their balconies.   The passions of the young
> are violent and short-lived; the vices of older men
> seldom range beyond an addiction to bowling, to ban-
> quets and 'socials, ' or clubs where large sums change
> hands on the fall of a card.   [Stuart Gilbert trans.]

As the plague begins to take over the city, certain traditional
urban functions deteriorate, but a new sense of community
emerges in the city.   The Parisian visitor to Oran, Ram-
bert, is caught in the city when the gates are closed, and

though he at first wants to escape, he gradually becomes part
of the new community: "Until now I always felt a stranger in
this town, and that I'd no concern with you people.   But now
that I've seen what I have seen, I know that I belong here
whether I want it or not.   This business is everybody's business. " What Camus suggests, in fact, is that the very crisis
of the plague galvanizes the city into a living community.
The result is not the heavenly city, but rather the rural virtues infused into the urban setting--a reversal indeed. Crisis, in other words, is not necessarily an evil; it may instead be an opportunity and one that to be realized requires
those rural virtues extolled by Goldsmith.

        Richard Wright, the father of modern American black
literature, has Cross Damon, the main character of The Outsider, paint a terribly bleak picture of the contemporary city.

        Few are the people who know the meaning of what
        they are living through, who even have an inkling
        of what is happening to them.   That's the big
        trouble with history.... Keep that point in mind
        while I remind you of what is happening in the great
        cities of the earth today-Chicago, Detroit, Pitts-
        burgh, London, Manchester, Paris, Tokyo, Hong
        Kong, and the rest.   These cities are, for the most
        part, vast pools of human misery, networks of raw
        human nerves exposed without benefit of illusion or
        hope to the new, godless world wrought by indus-
        trial man.   Industrial life plus a rampant capital-
        ism have blasted the lives of men in these cities;
        those who are lucky enough not to be hungry are
        ridden with exquisite psychological sufferings. The
        people of these cities are lost; some of them are
        so lost that they no longer even know it, and they
        are the real lost ones.   They haunt the movies for
        distraction; they gamble; they depress their sensi-
        bilities with alcohol; or they seek strong sensations
        or dull their sense of a meaningless existence....
                            (Perennial Library edition.)

Damon, as a black, is an outsider from white society, but in
his hatred he seeks to be completely outside--outside the city,
outside social intercourse.   And yet when dying he retracts,
recognizing the need for societal bonds.

        'The search can't be done alone.' He let his voice
        issue from a dry throat in which he felt death lurk-

ing. 'Never alone.... Alone a man is nothing....
Man is a promise that he must never break....
I wish I had some way to give the meaning of my
life to others.... To make a bridge from man to
man.... Starting from scratch every time is ...
no good. Tell them not to come down this road.'

Ralph Ellison picks up from Wright in his Invisible
Man. The hero is clearly an urbanite, living in New York
but having literally gone underground after failing to become
visible, to communicate. His failure and his retreat, however, have taught him an urban lesson.

No indeed, the world is just as concrete, ornery,
vile and sublimely wonderful as before, only now
I better understand my relation to it and it to me.
I've come a long way from those days when, full
of illusion, I lived a public life and attempted to
function under the assumption that the world was
solid and all the relationships therein. Now I know
men are different and that all life is divided and
that only in division is there true health....
Life is to be lived, not controlled; and humanity is
won by continuing to play in face of certain defeat.
Our fate is to become one, and yet many--This is
not prophecy, but description. [Signet edition.]

The novel ends with the hero's decision to return to the full
life of the city.

I'm shaking off the old skin and I'll leave it here
in the hole. I'm coming out, no less invisible
without it, but coming out nevertheless. And I
suppose it's damn well time. Even hibernations
can be overdone, come to think of it. Perhaps
that's my greatest social crime, I've overstayed
my hibernation, since there's a possibility that even
an invisible man has a socially responsible role to
play.

It is not insignificant, I think, that the Invisible Man's retreat, his place of hibernation before returning to social responsibility, is not the country but a basement under the city
of New York.

Using New Orleans as his setting, a new, young no-
velist, John William Corrington, has presented in The Upper

Hand a devastating vision of urban crime, violence, pollution,
and despair. He describes New Orleans in the image of
hell, and yet his hero, an ex-priest, begins to find his
spiritual salvation in that hell. Rejecting the formulaic pattern of a hero coming from the country to the city, seeing
its evils and perhaps picking up a little culture, and returning to the country to find salvation, Corrington sends his
hero to the city to find his humanity and his spiritual sanity.
The novel does not end with a retreat to the country but with
the hero entering a bar--and on the way to finding God. At
the end of the novel, the hero, viewing a street lamp and
"the soft light falling through a swerve of tumbling rain-
drops, " imagines the light is "composed of three radiant
circles.... But there is no definition, no clear edge between each circle, and the rain, the insects, a fitful wind
beginning to rise along the river, blowing in toward the
seething city--all of them merge and fuse into a fractured
unity" [Berkely edition]. This city of fractured unity, echo-
ing Ellison, and this allusion to the Trinity remind the hero
of the fractured unity and trinity of circles in the Ballantine
beer label: "Recalling with inordinate pleasure the Bethel Bar
in St. Peter Street where he can find a quiet glass of ale.
Ballantine on tap. Enough to cheer the living and the dead."
These are the last lines of the novel, and they recall the
line in the Apostles' Creed that asserts Christ will come to
"judge the living and the dead. " God is found in an ale can
in an urban bar--a far cry from Walden Pond.

The novelists I have cited here offer examples of a
new urban vision that contemporary literature is beginning to
project. It appears in such diverse writers as Saul Bellow,
Bernard Malamud, Robbe-Grillet, Anthony Powell, Robert
Lowell, and John Barth, to mention just a few. This new
urban vision, instead of rejecting the real city, is grappling
with it, attempting to focus it in terms of the heavenly city.
Urban crisis is now being viewed as urban opportunity for
self-realization and for the development of community. It
contains no simplistic belief that all's right with the city or
that well-wishing will bring the city into correspondence with
its ideal archetype. But the new urban vision does include
a belief in Samuel Johnson's conviction that "when a man is
tired of London, he is tired of life; for there is in London
all that life can afford. " And London is now everywhere.

NOTES ON CONTRIBUTORS

HERMAN BADILLO represents the Triborough District of New York City in the House of Representatives. He is the first Puerto Rican American to be elected to Congress. Among his congressional committee assignments is membership on the important House Education Committee. Congressman Badillo is an adjunct faculty member in the Division of Urban Education of Fordham University's School of Education. He is also a lawyer and former Bronx borough president.

MARIO FANTINI is a dean of the college of Education of New Paltz College of the State University of New York. Previously, Dr. Fantini served as education director of the Ford Foundation. His publications include: Designing Education for Tomorrow's Cities; The Disadvantages; Challenge to Education; Making Urban Schools Work; and Toward a Contract Curriculum.

JAMES FARMER is a noted human rights activist. He is a former assistant secretary of the Department of Health, Education and Welfare and national director of the Congress of Racial Equality (CORE). He has authored Freedom--When? and is currently working on his autobiography.

JOSEPH P. FITZPATRICK, S. J. is professor and chairman of the Sociology Department at Fordham University. His books include Puerto Rican Americans; The Meaning of Migration to the Mainland; The Analysis of Delinquent Behavior; Delinquent Behavior: A Definition of the Problem.

JOHN HOLT is an author, lecturer, teacher and critic of American Education. His books include: How Children Fail; How Children Learn; The Underachieving School; and What Do We Do on Monday?

CARL MARBURGER is New Jersey State Commissioner of Education. He served for many years as an educator in the Detroit public school system. Dr. Marburger was director of the Task Force on Disadvantaged Youth sponsored

145

by the United States Office of Education and was also
assistant commissioner of education.

SHELDON MARCUS is chairman of Fordham University's Division of Urban Education. He has served in the
New York City public school system as a teacher and administrator. He is the author of Father Coughlin: A Biography and the co-author of Conflicts in Urban Education.

RHODY McCOY is a member of the faculty of the
University of Massachusetts' College of Education. He was
formerly unit administrator of the Ocean Hill-Brownsville
Demonstration School District, Brooklyn, New York.

THOMAS R. PRESTON is director of the Division of
Humanities at the University of Tennessee at Chattanooga.
He has published many articles on 18th-century literature and
on literary theory and is teaching courses on the image of
the city in literature. He has just completed a book entitled
Not in Timon's Manner, a satire on 18th century England.

ALBERT SHANKER is president of the United Federation of Teachers and Vice President of the American Federation of Teachers. He is a member of the Executive Board
of the New York City Central Labor Council, the Board of
Directors of the League for Industrial Democracy, and the
Board of Trustees of the Center for Urban Education.

PERCY E. SUTTON is president of the Borough of
Manhattan. He is a lawyer, civil rights activist and co-
chairman of the National Conference of Black Elected Officials. Mr. Sutton is a former president of the New York
Branch of the NAACP.

JAMES R. TANNER is assistant superintendent for
curriculum and instruction for the Cleveland Public Schools.
He is a consultant and advisor to the United States Office of
Education. Dr. Tanner is a former member of the faculty
of Bowling Green State University.

PHILIP D. VAIRO is dean of the college of professional
studies at the University of Tennessee at Chattanooga. Formerly, he served as chairman of the Division of Curriculum and
Teaching at Fordham University. Among his numerous publications are: How To Teach Disadvantaged Youth and Urban Education: Problems and Prospects.

PRESTON WILCOX is director of Afram Associates, Inc. He served as chief consultant for the I. S. 201 complex and was a member of the faculty of Columbia University's School of Social Work. He is former director of the East Harlem Project and the Maria Lawton Center for Older People. He is chairman for the National Association for African American Education. Mr. Wilcox is the author of numerous publications.

INDEX

City College of New York, 104-105
civil rights, 11, 21, 79
Clark, Kenneth B., 90, 92
Clark plan, Washington, 82
class size, 14, 24
Cleaver, Eldridge, 94
Cleveland, public schools, 108; starving children in, 108-109
Coleman, James, 62, 64
Coleman Report, 58
community activism, 50
community control, 28-29, 50, 78, 85, 86, 112-113, 117-118, 119, 127-128; black caucuses, 35; community unions, 35; decentralization, 36, 37; de-re-centralization, 36; drug traffic, 33; Harlem I. S. 201, 30-32, 37, 38; hospitals, 36, 128; housing, 33-34; independent black schools, 36; labor unions, 35, 40; literature on, 36-37; as national movement, 36-37; NYC Board of Education, 30, 31; racism, of the system, 30-31; requisites for change, 31-33; school as political instrument, 34-35; welfare allowances, 33; and white Establishment, 37-40
community schools, combined, 64; total, 124
community unions, 35
compensatory education, 116-117
Conant, James B., 214
consumerism, 50
CORE, 40
Cronbach, Lee J., 132

Dark Ghetto, 92
day-care centers, 64
Death at an Early Age, 90-91
decentralization, 11, 19-20, 26, 36, 37, 118-119
de-re-centralization, 36
desegregation, 51, 117-118
diplomas, high school, 44, 84, 101
discipline, 27-28, 32
discrimination, racial, 53-54, 89-91, 92-93, 94-95, 98
dropout rates, 44
drug traffic, 33

ecology movement, 50
education: anti-urban bias, 11, 21; automated school, 124; big lie, 46; bilingual, 101-102; black teachers, 84-85; career oriented, 123-124; class size, 14; community control, 50, 85, 86, 117-118, 119; compensatory, 116-117; corporal punishment, 32; de-

education (cont.)
centralization, 11, 19-20, 118-119; desegregation, 51,
117-118; diplomas, high school, 44, 84, 101; dismantling of public systems, 19, 21; evolution of, in
U. S., 47-48; federal control, 19; ghetto children, 96-
97; illiteracy, 82-83; integration, 80-81, 86, 91;
minorities, 8, 11, 12, 30, 31, 35, 49-50, 82, 83,
84, 87; Montessori, 124; multi-culture school, 124-
125; open classroom, 123; parallel-schools, 120-121;
performance contract, 20, 113, 125; per-pupil expenditures, 91, 97; in pluralistic society, 87-88, 116;
and power structure, 9, 11, 12, 45-46, 48, 50;
principals' role, 10, 14, 15, 16; public-schools-of-
choice plan, 122-123, 125; quality of, 80, 81, 115,
118, 119; racial discrimination, 89-91, 92-93, 98;
reform ground-rules, 121-122; school boards, 9, 13,
14, 15, 19, 61, 118, 120; school-within a school
plan, 123; segregation, 80-81, 86, 91, 112; and the
social order, 111-112; standardized tests, 83-84;
state control, 9; state-wide systems, 19; suburbs, 95,
112; superintendents' role, 9, 10, 62; teachers, 10,
11, 12, 13, 15, 16-17, 18, 35, 37, 38, 82, 84-85,
86-87, 120, 122; total community school, 124; traditional, 123; voucher system, 20-21, 53, 86-87, 113,
119, 120, 125; worldwide, 51
education, higher: administrators' training, 61-62;
equalizing opportunity, 51-52; external degrees, 53;
independent black institutions, 36; leadership training, 48-49; minorities, 44, 52-53; new experiments
in, 53; open admissions, 51; racial discrimination,
53-54
education, parochial: as alternate system, 77; blacks,
70, 71, 75-77, 78; Catholic immigrants, 68-69, 70,
72, 76, 77, 104; community control, 78; culture, 71-
73; financial pressures, 68, 76; intercultural communication training, 72-73; Jewish immigrants, 69,
104; New York Archdiocese, 70, 71; Puerto Ricans,
70-73, 75, 76, 77, 78; religious personnel, 68, 74,
75, 76, 78; role of, 74; secular function of, 69, 75;
teaching methods, 73-74; youth revolt, 73-74
education, urban: administration, 48, 61-62, 63, 64,
132; alternate schools, 113; blacks, 58-59; busing,
130-131; career development, 132-133; community
control, 112-113, 127-128; culture of poverty, 58;
equal opportunities, 62; government, 64-65, 66; high
schools, 114; male teachers, 132; open housing, 130-
131; per-pupil expenditures, 131; principals, 61, 63;
private schools, 120-121; property taxation, 131;

education, urban (cont.)
  reading, teaching of, 131-132; vs. rural education,
  129; segregation, 130; separate but equal, 131; state/
  regional authority, 64-65; students, 57-58; suburbs,
  55, 56; tax equalization, 56-57; teacher-pupil ratio,
  131; teachers training, 128-129; teachers, 59-61, 62-
  63, 95-96, 97-99, 113-114, 132; and the urban dilemma, 55-56; and urban universities, 129-130
Edwards, E. Babette, 30
Ellison, Ralph, 93
equal opportunities, 62
Euclid Citizen's Council, Ohio, 110-111
external degrees, 53
extra-curricular activity, 49

Fantini, Mario, 115-126
Farmer, James, 79-88
Ferguson, Herman, 31
Fitzpatrick, Joseph P., 67-78
Ford Foundation, 116
Fordham University, 74, 127
Fox, Monsignor, 73
Freedom Schools, 120
free schools, 64

Gary, Indiana, 125
ghetto children, 96-97
ghetto ethic, 96
good neighbor policy, 106
Great Cities School Improvement Program, 116
Gregory, Dick, 94

Haaren High School, 104
Handlin, Oscar, 94-95
Harlem I.S. 201, 30-32, 37, 38
Harlem Preparatory School, 53, 120
Herndon, James, 91-92
Higher Horizons Program, 116
high schools, urban, 114
Hillel, Rabbi, 88
Holt, John, 1-8
hospitals, community control of, 36, 128
housing, 33-34, 105, 130-131
How Children Fail, 2
How Children Learn, 1
Hull, Bill, 2

illiteracy, 82-83
immigrants, Catholic, 68-69, 70, 72, 76, 77, 104;
   Jewish, 69, 104
income gap, for blacks, 53-54
Indians, American, 34, 35, 46, 50
Infant Schools, British, 25, 123
Institute for Human Development, 73
Institute of Intercultural Communication, 72-73
integration, 26, 80-81, 86, 91
Invisible Man, The, 93
Italian-American Veterans Club, 88

Jencks, Christopher, 64
Jensen, A. R., 37, 83, 85
Jewish Teachers for Community Control, 40
Jones Act, 102

Kent State University, 35
Kerner Report, 66
King, Martin Luther, 88
Kohl, Herbert, 92
Kozol, Jonathan, 90, 91

labor unions, 35, 40
leadership training, 48-49
Los Angeles Board of Education, 79-80
Louisiana State University at New Orleans, 130

McClure, William, 130
McCoy, Rhody, 22-29
Malcolm X, 46
Mao Tse-tung, 46
Marburger, Carl, 55-66
Marcus, Sheldon, 89-100
Marland, Sidney P., Jr., 133
mathematics, teaching of, 44, 73
Medgar Evers College, 53
Middle class, 49, 50, 62-63, 74, 82, 84, 95-96, 97-
   99, 130, 131
minority groups, 8, 11, 12, 26, 30, 31, 32, 34, 35,
   44, 49-50, 52-53, 82, 83, 84, 87
Montessori method, 24, 124
More Effective Schools Program, 116
multi-culture school, 124-125

NAACP, 40
National Association for African American Education, 35
National Educational Association, 10, 13, 35

156